We Owe it to Our Children

Time to Take Back Our Country!

Danny Cox

I0145003

2 Chronicles 7:14King James Version (KJV)

14 If my people, which are called by my name, shall humble themselves, and pray, and seek my face, and turn from their wicked ways; then will I hear from heaven, and will forgive their sin, and will heal their land.

Mom and Dad, I dedicate this book to you. You taught me anything worth having is worth working for. You taught me that even though it is often not easy, you have to stand for what is right, no matter the cost. Hopefully my children will learn the same from me. I love you both, and am so very proud to call you Mom and Dad.

Danny

Forward

The idea for this book started in 1983. I was Chief of Police in a small town in rural Alabama. The best job I ever had! We had a series of burglaries, the majority of which were at the home of senior citizens. People who were on fixed incomes and could afford it the least.

After an investigation I made an arrest in the case which ended solving 13 burglaries, 12 of which were senior citizens. Not all of them were in our city limits, but were in our general area. The young "man" I arrested could not come up with bail money which meant he had to remain in jail until his trial. Because all these burglaries were committed before he was caught they all counted as his first offense. The Judge gave him 3 years, which meant he was eligible for parole in 2. By the time the case was over he had been in county jail for a year and a half. The decision was made by the State to not even transfer him to prison since it was so close to his release date. He ended up spending 24 months in county jail for 13 burglaries! He never saw the inside of a prison.

Every Monday thru Friday we had an event at our Civic Center for senior citizens, where they could come have lunch and fellowship with each other. It was a great thing to do. For some of those attending it was the only way they would get a good home cooked meal. The only way they would have companionship.

Shortly after the conviction I happened to go visit the seniors at lunch. They were very upset this person was not punished worse than he was. They asked how? Why?

I thought about it for a moment, then told them it was their fault. You can imagine the shock that caused a room full of senior citizens. I went on to explain. The reason our country is in the shape it's in is because main stream America has been so busy working and raising a family we have allowed a minority to dictate the direction our country is headed. I am not talking about a racial minority! I'm talking about a socialist, Marxist, liberal minority. They have produced a culture that is bringing about the downfall of this once great nation. Liberals have gained control of the media, academia, the government, the legal profession, and unfortunately too many pulpits.

As I told that group it is up to us ordinary citizens to decide enough is enough, it's time to take a stand. It will require work, it won't be easy, but we owe it to our God, our Children and our Forefather's. My prayer is this book will help inspire people to start standing up for what they believe in. To make a difference.

If you aren't asking yourself who does he think he is writing this book? Or what does he think makes him smart enough to write this book? Don't worry you will ask those questions before you finish reading. That is okay. I have been asking myself that same question since 1983 when God first put it on my heart.

More than that you would never believe all the excuses I made for not writing it. God just put it on my heart to write it. I gave Him every excuse why He should choose someone more qualified. More talented. He just would not let me forget it. For 32 years this book has been on my heart and mind. I had a lot done on the original manuscript in 2009, but lost it to a house fire.

When I finally gave in and started the manuscript again I let my wife Jean read parts of it as I do all the books I write. She would read it, bring it back to me and ask if I was sure I wanted to write that. I always the same. No I don't, but someone has to.

That is truly the way I feel in my heart. It is time. It is past time. Someone has to stand up and say the hard things. Not out of hate or malice, but out of love. Love for my God, my Family, my country and my fellow man.

I want America to be great again. I want once again for America to be a beacon on the hill for all the world to see. I want to hear well done my true and faithful servant when I arrive in Heaven. More importantly I want to be joined in Heaven by each of you. So if the book offends you, I can't help it. I only wrote what was put on my heart, and as you will see I backed it all up by The Scriptures.

May God Bless you all, and May God Bless America!

Table of Contents

Chapter 1 – It Begins With You!

George Washington

1st U.S. President

"While we are zealously performing the duties of good citizens and soldiers, we certainly ought not to be inattentive to the higher duties of religion. To the distinguished character of Patriot, it should be our highest glory to add the more distinguished character of Christian."

--The Writings of Washington, pp. 342-343.

If we are to put America back on the right track it must begin with you. You have to do it. You can't wait on someone else. It won't be easy, as my parents burned into my brain growing up, nothing worth having ever is. It won't happen overnight, we didn't allow our country to get into this place overnight. It has to start with you, it has to begin at home.

There is a country song that says:

Drivin' through town just my boy and me

With a "Happy Meal" in his booster seat

Knowin' that he couldn't have the toy 'til his nuggets were gone.

A green traffic light turned straight to red

I hit my brakes and mumbled under my breath.

His fries went a flyin', and his orange drink covered his lap

Well, then my 4 year old said a 4 letter word

It started with "S" and I was concerned

So I said, "Son, now where'd you learn to talk like that?"

Chorus:

He said, I've been watching you, dad ain't that kool?

I'm your buckaroo, I want to be like you.

And eat all my food and grow as tall as you are.

We got cowboy boots and camo pants

Yeah, we're just alike, hey, ain't we dad

I want to do everything you do.

So I've been watching you.

We got back home and I went to the barn

I bowed my head and I prayed real hard

Said, "Lord, please help me help my stupid self."

Just this side of bedtime later that night

Turnin' on my son's Scooby-doo nightlight.

He crawled out of bed and he got down on his knees.

He closed his little eyes, folded his little hands

Spoke to God like he was talkin' to a friend.

And I said, "Son, now where'd you learn to pray like that?"

Chorus:

He said, I've been watching you, dad ain't that kool?

I'm your buckaroo; I want to be like you.

And eat all my food and grow as tall as you are.

We like fixin' things and holding moma's hand

Yeah, we're just alike, hey, ain't we dad.

I want to do everything you do; so I've been watching you.

With tears in my eyes I wrapped him in a hug.

Said, "My little bear is growin' up."

And he said, "But when I'm big I'll still know what to do."

Chorus:

'cause I've been watching you, dad ain't that kool?

I'm your buckaroo; I want to be like you.

And eat all my food and grow as tall as you are.

By then I'll be strong as superman

We'll be just alike, hey, won't we dad

When I can do everything you do.

'cause I've been watchin' you.

That song by Rodney Adkins says much more eloquently than I have the talent to say our children learn from us. Not as much by what we try to teach them as they do by observing us.

I'm not perfect. I didn't raise perfect children. Unfortunately they learned a lot of bad habits by watching me. They had their problems growing up, but they turned out to be good hard working young adults in spite of my and their Mother's mistakes. I look back now and I see where had I been a better parent, a better husband, a better Christian their lives would have been so much better.

We tell our children not to lie. We tell them honesty is the best policy, but then they see us call in sick to work when we aren't really sick. Or we tell them to answer the phone and say we aren't there or we are in the shower, or any number of excuses, and we've just taught them to lie. Or we spend money we don't want our spouse to know about and we say don't tell your Mom or Dad, and we've just taught them to lie.

We teach them not to steal, yet look at the following employee theft statistics.

Amount stolen annually from U.S. businesses by employees $50,000,000,000

Percent of annual revenues lost to theft or fraud 7 %

Percent of employees who have stolen at least once from their employer 75 %

Percent of employees who have stolen at least twice from their employer 37.5 %

Percent of all business bankruptcies caused by employee theft 33 %

Those are some staggering statistics. 75% of all American workers have admitted to stealing at least once from their employers. That means every good or service we purchase is higher just because of employee theft, not counting theft or fraud by those other than employees.

So the next time you think of bringing something home from work, remember your child is watching. You've just taught your child it is ok to steal.

The next time you are at work and you think of taking something home that doesn't belong to you remember your child is watching you. Remember God is watching you. He said "Thou shalt not steal." Nowhere behind that was an asterisk and unless it's from the company you work for.

It is all about honesty, integrity, discipline. It is about staying true to God's Word, and leading by example to your children and your spouse.

When you are driving with your child in your car do you obey all the traffic laws? I must confess I didn't. What did I teach my children? These things may sound trivial to the casual reader, but please really think about it. You are teaching your child it is ok to break the rules. Then if you are caught by the police with your child in the car, do you admit you are wrong, or do you try to lie your way out of it? If you try to lie your way out of it, now you have taught your child it ok to break the rules, and if you are caught lie about it.

We must exhibit self-discipline to teach discipline. One of the biggest problems America faces is lack of discipline. I hate to admit it, but unfortunately it is true. Look at the riots in Baltimore. The riots in Ferguson. Look at the news reports from Panama City Beach, Florida during spring break. It's not a race issue, not a class issue, it is a discipline issue. It is an obedience to God issue. Please don't get me wrong. I didn't do everything right growing up. I certainly didn't do everything right as a parent, and I don't do everything right now, but I try.

There was a time if a parent didn't teach discipline at home, the teacher, or principal, or coach would at school. I had my back side torn up many times by a Coach with a paddle. It didn't permanently scar me. If they couldn't the police, the jails, and the courts would. We have allowed liberals to take that ability away. No matter what your position is on corporal punishment for your children, God's position is very plain.

Proverbs 13:24King James Version (KJV)

24 He that spareth his rod hateth his son: but he that loveth him chasteneth him betimes.

Proverbs 23:13-15King James Version (KJV)

13 Withhold not correction from the child: for if thou beatest him with the rod, he shall not die.

14 Thou shalt beat him with the rod, and shalt deliver his soul from hell.

15 My son, if thine heart be wise, my heart shall rejoice, even mine.

Hebrews 12:5-11King James Version (KJV)

5 And ye have forgotten the exhortation which speaketh unto you as unto children, My son, despise not thou the chastening of the Lord, nor faint when thou art rebuked of him: 6 For whom the Lord loveth he chasteneth, and scourgeth every son whom he receiveth.

7 If ye endure chastening, God dealeth with you as with sons; for what son is he whom the father chasteneth not? 8 But if ye be without chastisement, whereof all are partakers, then are ye bastards, and not sons.

9 Furthermore we have had fathers of our flesh which corrected us, and we gave them reverence: shall we not much rather be in subjection unto the Father of spirits, and live?

10 For they verily for a few days chastened us after their own pleasure; but he for our profit, that we might be partakers of his holiness.

11 Now no chastening for the present seemeth to be joyous, but grievous: nevertheless afterward it yieldeth the peaceable fruit of righteousness unto them which are exercised thereby.

If you remember earlier I said I didn't do everything right as a parent. I still don't. When I was a young parent I couldn't believe God said sparing the rod meant I didn't love my child. Now that I am older and wiser I can see the wisdom in God's Words. I hardly ever used corporal punishment on our children. My children paid the price for it. I spared the rod because it tore me up emotionally to strike my children. So it was very, very rare I did.

I look back now and see how selfish that was. I didn't give them what they needed because it hurt me. I didn't follow God's Word. I didn't follow what my Mom and Dad did to me that obviously worked. I certainly didn't follow what my Grandparents did to my parents that obviously worked.

Do you see a trend? I know it isn't just in my family this trend exists. With each generation children are getting more disrespectful to any authority. Parental, School, Law Enforcement, any authority. Is it a coincidence the further away we get from Biblical teaching the more children are rebelling against authority? Even God's authority?

It is the same as a sinner such as I rebelling against God's authority. Sometimes He must discipline me to get me back on the straight and narrow. Now that I am older and hopefully wiser, I just look towards the Heavens and say yes sir, I hear you God. Doesn't mean I enjoy it. Doesn't mean I like it. I do however love that He loves me enough to discipline me when I need it.

God thinks discipline and self-discipline is so important I have found more than 80 Bible verses that speak about it so far. I suspect I will find many more. A couple of my favorites are:

Hebrews 12:7

Endure hardship as discipline; God is treating you as his children. For what children are not disciplined by their father?

Proverbs 3:11-13King James Version (KJV)

11 My son, despise not the chastening of the Lord; neither be weary of his correction:

12 For whom the Lord loveth he correcteth; even as a father the son in whom he delighteth.

13 Happy is the man that findeth wisdom, and the man that getteth understanding.

Proverbs 5:22-23New International Version (NIV)

22 The evil deeds of the wicked ensnare them;

the cords of their sins hold them fast.

23 For lack of discipline they will die,

led astray by their own great folly.

I am certainly not advocating child abuse. I am only saying follow God's plan. Teach your children discipline out of love for them. Do it by example, time outs, taking privileges away, and yes if need be with a belt or a switch. Just don't do it out of anger, wait until the anger subsides and do it out of love. They will thank you for it one day.

Chapter 2 - Yes, There is a Hell

Patrick Henry

Ratifier of the U.S. Constitution

"It cannot be emphasized too strongly or too often that this great nation was founded, not by religionists, but by Christians; not on religions, but on the gospel of Jesus Christ. For this very reason peoples of other faiths have been afforded asylum, prosperity, and freedom of worship here."

--The Trumpet Voice of Freedom: Patrick Henry of Virginia, p. iii.

"The Bible ... is a book worth more than all the other books that were ever printed."

--Sketches of the Life and Character of Patrick Henry, p. 402.

There is a prominent Evangelist who is saying there is no Hell. That the Jesus he worships is so compassionate he would never condemn anyone to Hell. I wonder where these people get this stuff. They must have a different Bible than I.

Just a few Scriptures from the New Testament because these tickle your ear feel good Preachers like to use primarily the New Testament.

Matthew 5:22

But I say unto you, That whosoever is angry with his brother without a cause shall be in danger of the judgment: and whosoever shall say to his brother, Raca, shall be in danger of the council: but whosoever shall say, Thou fool, shall be in danger of hell fire.

Matthew 5:29

And if thy right eye offend thee, pluck it out, and cast it from thee: for it is profitable for thee that one of thy members should perish, and not that thy whole body should be cast into hell.

Matthew 5:30

And if thy right hand offend thee, cut it off, and cast it from thee: for it is profitable for thee that one of thy members should perish, and not that thy whole body should be cast into hell.

Matthew 10:28

And fear not them which kill the body, but are not able to kill the soul: but rather fear him which is able to destroy both soul and body in hell.

Matthew 11:23

And thou, Capernaum, which art exalted unto heaven, shalt be brought down to hell: for if the mighty works, which have been done in thee, had been done in Sodom, it would have remained until this day.

Matthew 16:18

And I say also unto thee, That thou art Peter, and upon this rock I will build my church; and the gates of hell shall not prevail against it.

Matthew 23:15

Woe unto you, scribes and Pharisees, hypocrites! for ye compass sea and land to make one proselyte, and when he is made, ye make him twofold more the child of hell than yourselves.

Matthew 23:33

Ye serpents, ye generation of vipers, how can ye escape the damnation of hell?

Luke 16:23

And in hell he lift up his eyes, being in torments, and seeth Abraham afar off, and Lazarus in his bosom.

2 Peter 2:4

For if God spared not the angels that sinned, but cast them down to hell, and delivered them into chains of darkness, to be reserved unto judgment;

Revelation 1:18

I am he that liveth, and was dead; and, behold, I am alive for evermore, Amen; and have the keys of hell and of death.

Revelation 6:8

And I looked, and behold a pale horse: and his name that sat on him was Death, and Hell followed with him. And power was given unto them over the fourth part of the earth, to kill with sword, and with hunger, and with death, and with the beasts of the earth.

Revelation 20:13

And the sea gave up the dead which were in it; and death and hell delivered up the dead which were in them: and they were judged every man according to their works.

Revelation 20:14

And death and hell were cast into the lake of fire. This is the second death.

So as one can plainly see there is a Hell. Now as for Jesus being too compassionate to send anyone there.

Luke 12:51-53King James Version (KJV)

51 Suppose ye that I am come to give peace on earth? I tell you, Nay; but rather division: 52 For from henceforth there shall be five in one house divided, three against two, and two against three. 53 The father shall be divided against the son, and the son against the father; the mother against the daughter, and the daughter against the mother; the mother in law against her daughter in law, and the daughter in law against her mother in law.

Matthew 7:21-23King James Version (KJV)

21 Not every one that saith unto me, Lord, Lord, shall enter into the kingdom of heaven; but he that doeth the will of my Father which is in heaven. 22 Many will say to me in that day, Lord, Lord, have we not prophesied in thy name? and in thy name have cast out devils? and in thy name done many wonderful works? 23 And then will I profess unto them, I never knew you: depart from me, ye that work iniquity.

I am telling you friends, if you aren't in a Bible believing Church that teaches the Bible, the entire Bible get out! We may very well be living in the final days, make sure you are in a Church that is using sound Biblical teachings.

We have too many Churches now who are simply "tickling the ears", telling people what they want to hear. Woe be unto those Pastors. There will come a day they will pay a tremendous price. Those who teach the message of "God wants you to be happy, healthy, wealthy, etc… are simply not teaching what Jesus said. Sure He would like that if not for man's sinful nature. Jesus wants you to spend eternity in Heaven with Him. He knows more than we do what our needs are in order to live the life we need to live to get there and help others get there.

Jesus warned us many times we would have troubles.

Matthew 10:21-23King James Version (KJV)

21 And the brother shall deliver up the brother to death, and the father the child: and the children shall rise up against their parents, and cause them to be put to death. 22

And ye shall be hated of all men for my name's sake: but he that endureth to the end shall be saved.

23 But when they persecute you in this city, flee ye into another: for verily I say unto you, Ye shall not have gone over the cities of Israel, till the Son of man be come.

Matthew 24:8-10King James Version (KJV)

8 All these are the beginning of sorrows. 9 Then shall they deliver you up to be afflicted, and shall kill you: and ye shall be hated of all nations for my name's sake. 10 And then shall many be offended, and shall betray one another, and shall hate one another.

Luke 6:21-23King James Version (KJV)

21 Blessed are ye that hunger now: for ye shall be filled. Blessed are ye that weep now: for ye shall laugh. 22 Blessed are ye, when men shall hate you, and when they shall separate you from their company, and shall reproach you, and cast out your name as evil, for the Son of man's sake.

23 Rejoice ye in that day, and leap for joy: for, behold, your reward is great in heaven: for in the like manner did their fathers unto the prophets.

John 12:24-26 King James Version (KJV)

24 Verily, verily, I say unto you, Except a corn of wheat fall into the ground and die, it abideth alone: but if it die, it bringeth forth much fruit. 25 He that loveth his life shall lose it; and he that hateth his life in this world shall keep it unto life eternal.

26 If any man serve me, let him follow me; and where I am, there shall also my servant be: if any man serve me, him will my Father honour.

John 15:18-20King James Version (KJV)

18 If the world hate you, ye know that it hated me before it hated you. 19 If ye were of the world, the world would love his own: but because ye are not of the world, but I have chosen you out of the world, therefore the world hateth you.

20 Remember the word that I said unto you, The servant is not greater than his lord. If they have persecuted me, they will also persecute you; if they have kept my saying, they will keep yours also.

Matthew 19:24King James Version (KJV)

24 And again I say unto you, It is easier for a camel to go through the eye of a needle, than for a rich man to enter into the kingdom of God.

Look at the persecution the Disciples and the early Church endured. If we live our life as a devoted Bible believing Jesus loving Christian we are still going to have troubles in this life, but we have a Savior to help us thru those times!

Friends the Church is in desperate need of a Revival. We have Churches who have invited Muslim Imams into the Pulpit to speak and read from the Quran. We have Churches who are participating in same sex marriages. We have Churches who arc ordaining homosexuals as Ministers, Deacons and Elders. We have Churches that have little or no problem with abortion. We have been warned of these days!

2 Timothy 4:2-5King James Version (KJV)

2 Preach the word; be instant in season, out of season; reprove, rebuke, exhort with all long suffering and doctrine. 3 For the time will come when they will not endure sound doctrine; but after their own lusts shall they heap to themselves teachers, having itching ears;

4 And they shall turn away their ears from the truth, and shall be turned unto fables.

5 But watch thou in all things, endure afflictions, do the work of an evangelist, make full proof of thy ministry.

2 Peter 2:1-5King James Version (KJV)

1 But there were false prophets also among the people, even as there shall be false teachers among you, who privily shall bring in damnable heresies, even denying the Lord that bought them, and bring upon themselves swift destruction.

2 And many shall follow their pernicious ways; by reason of whom the way of truth shall be evil spoken of.

3 And through covetousness shall they with feigned words make merchandise of you: whose judgment now of a long time lingereth not, and their damnation slumbereth not.

4 For if God spared not the angels that sinned, but cast them down to hell, and delivered them into chains of darkness, to be reserved unto judgment;

5 And spared not the old world, but saved Noah the eighth person, a preacher of righteousness, bringing in the flood upon the world of the ungodly;

Galatians 1:6-9King James Version (KJV)

6 I marvel that ye are so soon removed from him that called you into the grace of Christ unto another gospel:

7 Which is not another; but there be some that trouble you, and would pervert the gospel of Christ.

8 But though we, or an angel from heaven, preach any other gospel unto you than that which we have preached unto you, let him be accursed. 9 As we said before, so say I now again, if any man preach any other gospel unto you than that ye have received, let him be accursed.

Matthew 15:8-14King James Version (KJV)

8 This people draweth nigh unto me with their mouth, and honoureth me with their lips; but their heart is far from me. 9 But in vain they do worship me, teaching for doctrines the commandments of men. 10 And he called the multitude, and said unto them, Hear, and understand:

11 Not that which goeth into the mouth defileth a man; but that which cometh out of the mouth, this defileth a man. 12 Then came his disciples, and said unto him, Knowest thou that the Pharisees were offended, after they heard this saying?

13 But he answered and said, Every plant, which my heavenly Father hath not planted, shall be rooted up. 14

Let them alone: they be blind leaders of the blind. And if the blind lead the blind, both shall fall into the ditch.

Jude 4-5King James Version (KJV)

4 For there are certain men crept in unawares, who were before of old ordained to this condemnation, ungodly men, turning the grace of our God into lasciviousness, and denying the only Lord God, and our Lord Jesus Christ.

5 I will therefore put you in remembrance, though ye once knew this, how that the Lord, having saved the people out of the land of Egypt, afterward destroyed them that believed not.

Wake up Brothers and Sisters! We are running out of time!

You may be asking why I included so much Scripture in this chapter. It is because I believe this is such an important topic! I am not the only one, Scripture is full of warnings about this. One of the Preachers I admire most says we have more Churches than ever before. More Bibles in print than ever before, and we are in more trouble than ever before! Every time I hear him say it I must say Amen!

Pastors, preach the Word of God. Don't simply "tickle the ears." Your flock will pay a heavy price if you do. According to the Scriptures you will pay an even heavier price.

We need a new Billy Graham. Someone who will get out and shake this country up! Someone with the true anointing of God and a passion to spread his Word. Not one of the TV Preachers who Preach only the feel good messages, live in multimillion dollar mansions, have their own airplanes and fleets of expensive cars.

We need a true man of God who cares more about helping start a revival in this country than lining his or her own pocket. Perhaps Franklin Graham will be that person. Franklin Graham does a lot of good. He preaches from the heart. He preaches the truth, not just tickles the ears. He isn't afraid to speak out about the sin issues facing America today.

The following is an excerpt from Franklin Graham's 2016 tour announcement. If there is I stop near you I highly recommend attending.

"I have heard from people all over America who believe that our nation is in trouble—morally, spiritually, and politically. But as attention turns to an election year, I do not believe that Republicans or Democrats (or any other party) can turn this nation around–only God can.

That's why in 2016 I will hold prayer rallies in the capitals of all 50 states. We're calling it the Decision America Tour, and it starts in January.

God hears the prayers of his people, so I'm calling on people of faith in every state to pray fervently for America and our leaders. I want to challenge Christians across our land to boldly live out and promote biblical principles at home, in public and at the ballot box. The only hope for this country is if the people of God are willing to take a stand for truth and righteousness.

To start the tour, we will hold prayer rallies at noon in these four cities:

January 5 Des Moines, IA (capitol building)

January 12 Tallahassee, FL (capitol building)

January 13 Baton Rouge, LA (location TBD)

January 19 Concord, NH (capitol building)

Decision America Tour will not endorse political candidates or legislation, and no candidates or current public officials will speak at any of the rallies. Instead, I will be sharing the life-changing truth of the Gospel of Jesus Christ in every state. Will you come out and pray with us?

Get more information about the other 46 states in the coming months at www.DecisionAmericaTour.com, a ministry of Billy Graham Evangelistic Association.

Please SHARE this with others.

Perhaps a Pastor at Gardendale First Baptist Church in Gardendale, Alabama, and no I am not a member there. Dr. Kevin Hamm is one of the Godliest men I have ever met. He is one of the finest Preachers I have ever heard. Pastor Kevin doesn't give a little 45 minute feel good sermonette. He passionately Preaches the Truth. If you want to hear a real Sermon you can access Pastor Kevin's Sermons on demand at this web address http://gfbc.com/

This is a brief bio of Pastor Kevin:

Dr. Kevin Hamm has been the Senior Pastor of Gardendale First Baptist Church in Gardendale, Alabama since April 2006. The church averages 3500 in worship and is consistently among the state leaders in baptisms.

Pastor Kevin often says, "God blesses a church that will worship Him in spirit and truth. Celebrative, passionate worship combined with Biblical, anointed preaching is a match made in Heaven!" He previously served nine years as the Senior Pastor of Valley View Church in Louisville, Kentucky which grew from 300 to 2700 weekly worshipers.

Pastor Kevin has the unique ability to hold an audience's attention by communicating God's Word with tremendous clarity and enthusiastic passion. He preaches all over including the Evangelism Conferences in Oklahoma, Georgia, Alabama, Kentucky, Arkansas, Tennessee and Mississippi. Pastor Kevin has served on the Executive Committee of the Southern Baptist Convention and as President of the Alabama Baptist Pastor's Conference. His articles have been published in Growing Churches, Leadership and Leader Life.

He has his B.A. from Western Kentucky University, M. Div. from Mid-America Theological Seminary and Doctor of Ministry degree from Southern Baptist Theological

Seminary. He married his wife, Kim, in 1987 and they have three daughters: Lindsey, Lauren and Kayla.

Pastor Kevin also speaks a lot at other Churches. You can access his schedule on the Church website.

Chapter 3 - Should A True Born Again Christian Vote Democrat?

Thomas Jefferson

3rd U.S. President, Drafter and Signer of the Declaration of Independence

"God who gave us life gave us liberty. And can the liberties of a nation be thought secure when we have removed their only firm basis, a conviction in the minds of the people that these liberties are of the Gift of God? That they are not to be violated but with His wrath? Indeed, I tremble for my country when I reflect that God is just; that His justice cannot sleep forever; That a revolution of the wheel of fortune, a change of situation, is among possible events; that it may become probable by Supernatural influence! The Almighty has no attribute which can take side with us in that event."

--Notes on the State of Virginia, Query XVIII, p. 237

I know this is going to get me in trouble, but the short answer is no. Before everyone starts throwing stones, I didn't say if you vote Democrat you aren't a Christian. What I am saying, at this point in history the Democratic Party does not reflect the Judeo Christian values and principles that made this country great. At this point in history, the Democratic Party is a Godless Party. From booing God and Israel at the 2012 Democratic National

Convention to the policies they support. Let's spend this chapter looking at the facts then you can draw your own conclusion.

Democrats on Abortion

Barack Obama:

Here is are some of his positions based on both his words and his votes as a State Senator and a U.S. Senator:

•Abortion on demand at every stage of pregnancy.

•Taxpayer funding of all abortions.

•Taxpayer funding of abortions overseas.

•Partial-birth abortions.

•Transporting minor girls across state lines to obtain secret abortions, circumventing home-state parental involvement laws.

•Infanticide of newborn babies who survive late-term abortions.

•The Freedom of Choice Act (FOCA), invalidating existing state and federal restrictions on abortion.

•Nomination of only judicial candidates who support Roe v. Wade and court-mandated policies of unlimited abortion.

•Human cloning, provided that all resulting human clones are subsequently killed and harvested for their useful parts.

Reacting to the recent Planned Parenthood videos, President Barack Obama's top spokesman Josh Earnest indicated Obama will definitely not agree with pro-life Republicans in Congress to revoke funding for the Planned Parenthood abortion business.

Harry Reid:

Voted NO on restricting UN funding for population control policies.

Voted NO on barring HHS grants to organizations that perform abortions.

This is from a fund raising letter he sent out in January of 2015 about fighting a Bill that banned abortions after 20 weeks:

"We knew it would be bad, Friends – but this Republican Congress surpassed our WORST NIGHTMARE:

On DAY ONE, Republican extremists in Congress launched their first major assault on women's health care – pushing a bill that would have BANNED abortions after 20 weeks of pregnancy. WORSE YET: The Republican bill would have refused care to rape victims until they report the horrific incident to authorities."

"We pushed back hard against these Republican extremists, but we know this won't be the last time they launch a DANGEROUS attack on life-saving women's care."

After abortionist Kermit Gosnell was convicted in 2013 of murdering infants after they were born, Reid said the lesson of the trial was that we need "clean and sterile" late-term abortion clinics.

Nancy Pelosi

When the videos came out about Planned Parenthood selling aborted Babies body parts this was her response:

House Minority Leader Nancy Pelosi (D-Calif.) joined calls for a federal investigation into the California-based anti-abortion group that sparked the Planned Parenthood hidden camera controversy.

"Let's have an investigation of those people who were trying to ensnare Planned Parenthood in a controversy that doesn't exist," Pelosi said.

In spite of the video showing them negotiating the price of the body parts, she went on to say this:

"Planned Parenthood has said that they have done nothing illegal," she said. "They do not ever charge, which would be illegal, for fetal tissue. They have only defrayed the cost of mailing that to someone, which is not breaking the law."

Some of her votes on Abortion:

Voted NO on banning federal health coverage that includes abortion.

Voted NO on restricting interstate transport of minors to get abortions.

Voted NO on making it a crime to harm a fetus during another crime.

Voted NO on banning partial-birth abortion except to save mother's life.

Voted NO on forbidding human cloning for reproduction & medical research.

Voted NO on funding for health providers who don't provide abortion info.

Voted NO on banning Family Planning funding in US aid abroad.

Voted NO on banning partial-birth abortions.

Voted NO on barring transporting minors to get an abortion.

The list could go on and on.

In addition she has said her support for unfettered abortion is consistent with her Catholic religion which the Church immediately disagreed with.

Debbie Wasserman Schultz

Like Nancy Pelosi, Debbie Wasserman Schultz has made some really wild statements in support of abortion. Let's look at her voting record first:

Voted NO on banning federal health coverage that includes abortion.

Voted NO on restricting interstate transport of minors to get abortions.

Emergency contraception for rape victims at all hospitals, Church owned hospitals included.

A New Hampshire journalist asked Sen. Rand Paul (R-Ky.) about his stance on abortion April 8. The 2016 presidential candidate retorted, "You go back and you ask Rep. Debbie Wasserman Schultz if she's OK with killing a seven-pound baby that is just not yet born yet."

Later that day she responded, "I support letting women and their doctors make this decision without government getting involved. Period," she wrote in a DNC statement. That sounds to me like she does!

I had information gathered about comments and votes from other Democratic leaders on abortion, but decided not to include them just to keep from boring the reader. From Elizabeth Warren, to Joe Biden, Chuck Schumer and more, but it is only more of the same.

Partial birth abortions? No problem! Late term abortions? No problem! Tax payer funded abortions? No problem! Minors having abortions without parental permission? No problem! 60,000,000 babies killed since Roe v. Wade? No problem!

Well let me tell you they may not have a problem with it, but one day they will stand before God and regret their advocacy for abortion!

Here are a few Scriptures that defend the prolife stance on abortion:

Jeremiah 1:4-5

Now the word of the LORD came to me, saying, "Before I formed you in the womb I knew you, and before you were born I consecrated you; I appointed you a prophet to the nations."

Isaiah 49:1,5

Listen to me, O coastlands, and give attention, you peoples from afar. The LORD called me from the womb, from the body of my mother he named my name... And now the LORD says, he who formed me from the womb to be his servant, to bring Jacob back to him; and that Israel might be gathered to him—for I am honored in the eyes of the LORD, and my God has become my strength.

Psalms 22:9-10

Yet you are he who took me from the womb; you made me trust you at my mother's breasts. On you was I cast from my birth, and from my mother's womb you have been my God.

Psalms 51:5

Behold, I was brought forth in iniquity, and in sin did my mother conceive me.

Genesis 25:22-26

The children struggled together within her, and she said, "If it is thus, why is this happening to me?" So she went to inquire of the LORD. And the LORD said to her, "Two nations are in your womb, and two peoples from within you shall be divided; the one shall be stronger than the other, the older shall serve the younger." When her days to give birth were completed, behold, there were twins in her womb. The first came out red, all his body like a hairy cloak, so they called his name Esau. Afterward his brother came out with his hand holding Esau's heel, so his name was called Jacob. Isaac was sixty years old when she bore them.

Judges 13:2-5

There was a certain man of Zorah, of the tribe of the Danites, whose name was Manoah. And his wife was barren and had no children. And the angel of the LORD appeared to the woman and said to her, "Behold, you are barren and have not borne children, but you shall conceive and bear a son. Therefore be careful and drink no wine or strong drink, and eat nothing unclean, for behold, you shall conceive and bear a son. No razor shall come upon his head, for the child shall be a Nazirite to God from the womb, and he shall begin to save Israel from the hand of the Philistines."

These are just a few of many. Do we really think God is not going to turn His back on America if we don't stop killing the innocent? 60,000,000 babies in 42 years, what a national disgrace.

Same Sex Marriage

Yes I know the polls say the majority of Americans support it. So? God doesn't. From the very beginning, from Adam and Eve on, Biblical marriage was between a man and a woman. That is until The Democratic Party and the U.S. Supreme Court decided they were more powerful than God. Would not want to be in their shoes one day soon.

In spite of President Obama's "evolution" on Gay marriage, I don't think God has changed His mind on a subject He was consistent on throughout The Holy Bible.

Leviticus 18:22

Thou shalt not lie with mankind, as with womankind: it [is] abomination.

Leviticus 20:13

If a man also lie with mankind, as he lieth with a woman, both of them have committed an abomination: they shall surely be put to death; their blood

Mark Chapter 10

6 But from the beginning of the creation God made them male and female.

7 For this cause shall a man leave his father and mother, and cleave to his wife;

8 And they twain shall be one flesh: so then they are no more twain, but one flesh.

9 What therefore God hath joined together, let not man put asunder. [shall be] upon them.

Romans Chapter 1

26 For this cause God gave them up unto vile affections: for even their women did change the natural use into that which is against nature:

27 And likewise also the men, leaving the natural use of the woman, burned in their lust one toward another; men with men working that which is unseemly, and receiving in themselves that recompence of their error

 which was meet.

28 And even as they did not like to retain God in [their] knowledge, God gave them over to a reprobate mind, to do those things which are not convenient;

1 Corinthians 7:2

Nevertheless, [to avoid] fornication, let every man have his own wife, and let every woman have her own husband

Jude 1:7

Even as Sodom and Gomorrha, and the cities about them in like manner, giving themselves over to fornication, and going after strange flesh, are set forth for an example, suffering the vengeance of eternal fire.

Speaking of Sodom and Gomorrha, if God would really do that to them do you not think He would pour out the same wrath on America?

Nancy Pelosi

House Minority Leader Rep. Nancy Pelosi, D-CA, says that same-sex "marriage" is perfectly "consistent" with Catholic Christianity. She summarized Catholic catechism as teaching support of gay 'marriage'. "The fact is, what we're taught was to respect people in our faith." Pelosi went on to criticize Rubio's opposition to gay 'marriage', explaining, "To say that [homosexual 'marriage'] endangers mainstream Christian thinking is so completely wrong."

These are some of her votes and strongly held opinions regarding same sex marriage issues:

Prohibit sexual-identity discrimination at schools which sounds good until you realize that is how transgender students are being allowed to use the bathroom of their choice.

NO on banning gay adoptions in DC

NO on Constitutional Amendment banning same-sex marriage

NO on constitutionally defining marriage as one-man-one-woman

Joe Biden

When asked by David Gregory about his views on same-sex marriage on Meet the Press on May 5, 2012, Biden noted that, while the President sets policy, Biden was "absolutely comfortable with the fact that men marrying men, women marrying women, and heterosexual men and women marrying another are entitled to the same exact rights, all the civil rights, all the civil liberties. And quite frankly, I don't see much of a distinction -- beyond that."

Please don't think I am saying we should be hateful or mean to homosexuals we shouldn't be. We should love them, we should pray for them, but we as Christians cannot support same sex marriage. It does go against God's Law.

It isn't only the Democratic policy on same sex marriage or abortion. Look at what their permissive liberal policies have accomplished in the cities and states the modern day Democratic Party has been in charge of. They are failing. Staggering crime rates, massive debt, low graduation rates, the list goes on.

Their attempts at solving poverty in the U.S. have only made poverty worse. The reason, their attempts reward immoral behavior.

2 Thessalonians 3:8-12King James Version (KJV)

8 Neither did we eat any man's bread for nought; but wrought with labour and travail night and day, that we might not be chargeable to any of you: 9 Not because we

have not power, but to make ourselves an ensample unto you to follow us.

10 For even when we were with you, this we commanded you, that if any would not work, neither should he eat. 11 For we hear that there are some which walk among you disorderly, working not at all, but are busybodies.

12 Now them that are such we command and exhort by our Lord Jesus Christ, that with quietness they work, and eat their own bread.

1 Timothy 5:8King James Version (KJV)

8 But if any provide not for his own, and specially for those of his own house, he hath denied the faith, and is worse than an infidel.

Ephesians 4:28King James Version (KJV)

28 Let him that stole steal no more: but rather let him labour, working with his hands the thing which is good, that he may have to give to him that needeth.

Democratic policies while maybe good intentioned have been destroying the inner cities and have now branched out to the suburbs. Many of these policies discourage women from marrying the Fathers of their Babies. Many encourage single women to have more babies so they get more in benefits. Many encourage people to stay home and not work because they can make more money off of government benefits than by working.

We should help these people, no matter their race, no matter if their problems are self-inflicted. The way the

Democratic Party has tried to help in the past has only hurt.

If we are going to truly help the people who are living in a cycle of poverty, we must begin to teach them discipline, self-discipline and pride in what they accomplish. With adding Biblical principles to the different government programs in my heart I believe we could change the face of poverty in 10 years. Just a few simple steps.

1. If you are getting welfare, section 8 housing, food stamps, or any government assistance and are physically able, you must work. Working will not cause you to lose your government assistance. As your income increases the amount of assistance will decrease.

2. If you are getting government assistance as a single parent and continue having children out of wedlock your amount of assistance drops instead of increasing.

3. If you are on government assistance you will be drug tested. The amount of assistance you receive will decrease with a positive test unless you go thru a government funded rehab program.

4. If you receive government assistance and don't have a High School Diploma or GED you will be required to get one.

5. Instead of being rewarded for being a single parent, the assistance programs will reward parents for staying together and raising their children together, and penalize those who don't.

Government assistance should be devised to lift people out of poverty. The way most of the programs are currently set up by the liberals in the Democratic Party they simply keep people in poverty and totally dependent on the government. This is not what Jesus taught!

Another couple of reasons I could never vote for the Democratic Party again, and don't see how a Christian should are two recent votes in the U.S. Senate. One of those votes was to withhold Federal funds from any city, town, county which violates Federal law by establishment of sanctuary areas for illegal immigrants.

These "Sanctuary Cities" are a direct violation of Federal law. Why would any Senator vote no on such a bill? Does anyone reading this think if a city or county refused to allow abortions the Democrats wouldn't be all over that city or county? They would send in the DOJ the FBI and any other Federal Agency they could. People would be arrested. They would be furious and never rest until it was changed. The Democratic Senators, all but two, voted against it.

The U.S. Senate failed to come up with the required 60 votes needed to move forward with the Sanctuary City Bill. The bill, S.2146, failed a procedural vote. The measure would have stripped federal funding for cities and other communities that do not honor requests from immigration officials to hold criminal illegal aliens in their jails

With a vote of 54-45, the measure failed to obtain the 60 votes necessary to end debate. Louisiana Senator Sen. David Vitter (R-LA) introduced the bill. Before the vote, Senator Vitter wrote, "Sanctuary cities and the associated violent crimes by illegal immigrants are reaching a critical point, and we cannot wait any longer to take action to protect Americans here at home. There is simply no incentive for these localities to enforce current immigration laws, and my legislation will make sure sanctuary cities are no longer rewarded for their failures to uphold the law. As the Senate debates the Stop Sanctuary Policies and Protect Americans Act, I urge my colleagues to remember Kate Steinle's vicious murder and the tens of thousands of crimes committed by illegal immigrants within our borders."

In a speech on the Senate floor, Texas Senator Sen. Ted Cruz (R-TX) said, "This class of illegal aliens has a special disregard and disdain for our nation's laws. And, too often, these offenders also have serious rap sheets…. We must send the message that defiance of our laws will no longer be tolerated—whether it's by the sanctuary cities themselves or the illegal reentry offenders that they harbor. The problem of illegal immigration in this country will never be solved until we demonstrate to the American people that we are serious about securing the border and enforcing our immigration laws. This bill is just a small step, but at least it's a small step in the right direction."

"Although these jurisdictions are more than happy — eager, even—to take federal dollars," Cruz continued, "they go out of their way to impede federal immigration enforcement by adopting policies that prohibit their law enforcement officers from cooperating with federal officers. Some of the jurisdictions even refuse to honor requests from the federal government to temporarily hold a criminal alien until federal officers can take custody of the individual."

There was one Republican who voted against it. I cannot understand how any sitting U.S. Senator could vote no on such a law. Maybe it was because the head of the Democratic Party, President Obama said he would veto the law if it made it to his desk. One more of many examples of enforcing the laws the President likes and refusing to enforce the ones he doesn't. Had I done that as a Police Chief I would have been arrested by the FBI.

The other bill I was referring too had to do with the Veterans Administration. Sen. Richard Blumenthal (D-Conn.), blocked an emergency bill, sponsored by Senator Marco Rubio (R-Fla.), that would make it easier to replace employees at the Veterans Administration healthcare centers. Democrats blocked a similar bill in May of 2014.

The American public has been appalled and demanded improvements in the V.A. system. Our Veterans continue to die, while waiting to be seen by the V.A. Why would Democrats block a bill that would make it easier to let an underperforming employee be terminated? We have seen where employees' low- level, mid-level, and high- level, have falsified records in regards to wait times. In most cases those employees are still employed. If you truly care about the healthcare crisis facing out Veterans, why would you block such a bill?

Perhaps this is why, The American Federation of Government Employees issued criticisms of the bill, the VA Accountability Act (S. 1082), "You simply can't fire your way to a solution," said AFGE President J. David Cox Sr. The Federal Employees Union doesn't like the bill. Unions almost exclusively support Democratic candidates. Maybe that's why the Democrats blocked the bill?

Chapter 4 - Get Involved in Choosing Your Government Leaders

John Quincy Adams

6th U.S. President

"The hope of a Christian is inseparable from his faith. Whoever believes in the divine inspiration of the Holy Scriptures must hope that the religion of Jesus shall prevail throughout the earth. Never since the foundation of the world have the prospects of mankind been more encouraging to that hope than they appear to be at the present time. And may the associated distribution of the Bible proceed and prosper till the Lord shall have made 'bare His holy arm in the eyes of all the nations, and all the ends of the earth shall see the salvation of our God' (Isaiah 52:10)."

--Life of John Quincy Adams, p. 248

At the beginning of every chapter I have started with a quote from one of our country's Founding Fathers. My reason is three fold. To show the Supreme Court got it wrong when they removed Prayer and Scripture from Schools and Public Institutions. To demonstrate the type of men and women we must elect as our government leaders.

To inspire the readers of this book to be that kind of leader in their personal and professional life.

When I first begin to study to become a preacher, one of my mentors, a man who I have a tremendous amount of respect for said I should always strive to keep politics out of the Pulpit. I love this man, I respect this man, but I 100% disagree with this man. We have a Christian duty to elect men and women who will govern using the Lord and His Holy Scripture as their guide.

We need to understand in order to truly change the direction of this country it must start at home, then at Church, in the community, in the schools, and grow from there. This chapter deals with making the change in schools and community. How many of you know who is on your local school board? How many know who is on your local City or Town Council? Your County Commission? Do you know how they have voted on issues important to you and your community? Do you know enough about them to have elected them in the first place? Do you know enough by their history of votes to say they should or should not be re-elected?

How about your local Municipal, County, or State Judges? Are you aware of how they have ruled in cases? Are they conservative or liberal?

We live in a time where all of that information is readily available. Start a small group in your Church, neighborhood or community. Make a list of the following:

School Board Members

Town or City Council Members

County Commission Members

State Education Members

State Prison Board Members

State Board of Pardons and Parole

Sate Members of House and Senate for your area

U.S. Senate and House Members for your area

City, County, State, and Federal Judges in your area

Divide the names up among your group members. Educate yourself. Find out everything you can about the people on your list. Get the minutes from City Council Meetings, School Board Meetings, etc… Check the voting records of your State and Federal House and Senate Members. They are readily available on the internet. Have they governed in a way consistent with Biblical principles? If not, find someone who will and vote the incumbent out.

Meet with your group once a month to compare notes and share information. Let these politicians know you are watching them. You and your group members will hold them accountable for their actions and votes on Election Day.

Talk to coworkers, family members, and friends, encourage them to start groups in their areas. Help them organize their groups. Band the local groups into a statewide group and on to a national group. To grow a group like this into a statewide or nationwide organization used to require a lot of time, money, and hard work. Now with the power of social media, with a lot of Prayer, a little self-discipline, and hard work this could quickly become the most active, most productive voting bloc in the Nation. You would be amazed at how quickly it could happen. Then, with God's help, we could put our country back on the right path.

Make a liberal mad. Start every meeting with a Prayer. End every meeting with a Prayer. Remember you aren't doing this for you. It is not about you. You are doing this for God, Country, and Family. You are doing this because it must be done if we are to save this country God richly blessed us with. As a country, we have turned our back on the One who gave us so much. We must take the following Scripture to heart:

2 Chronicles 7:14King James Version (KJV)

14 If my people, which are called by my name, shall humble themselves, and pray, and seek my face, and turn from their wicked ways; then will I hear from heaven, and will forgive their sin, and will heal their land.

We must hit our knees in anguish and Prayer and cry out to God to heal our land! We must encourage all those we come in contact with to do the same.

We are running out of time. God tells us none will know the day or time, but He did give us signs. The signs are there. I believe with all my heart, with everything in me, we can work together, we can pray together and we can inspire people to work with God's help to turn our country around. Will you do it?

Chapter 5 - United States Supreme Court Rulings That Put America in Conflict With God

John Jay

1st Chief Justice of the U.S. Supreme Court and President of the American Bible Society

"By conveying the Bible to people thus circumstanced, we certainly do them a most interesting kindness. We thereby enable them to learn that man was originally created and placed in a state of happiness, but, becoming disobedient, was subjected to the degradation and evils which he and his posterity have since experienced.

"The Bible will also inform them that our gracious Creator has provided for us a Redeemer, in whom all the nations of the earth shall be blessed; that this Redeemer has made atonement "for the sins of the whole world," and thereby reconciling the Divine justice with the Divine mercy has opened a way for our redemption and salvation; and that these inestimable benefits are of the free gift and grace of God, not of our deserving, nor in our power to deserve."

--In God We Trust—The Religious Beliefs and Ideas of the American Founding Fathers, p. 379.

2 Corinthians 3:17King James Version (KJV)

17 Now the Lord is that Spirit: and where the Spirit of the Lord is, there is liberty.

The Warren Supreme Court (1963) These are the men who banned School Prayer, and Bible reading in our public schools. Top Row L to R: Byron R. White, William J. Brennan, Potter Stewart, Arthur J. Goldberg. Seated L to R: Tom C. Clark, Hugo L. Black, Earl Warren, William O. Douglas, John M. Harian

Roe V. Wade Supreme Court - Chief Justice Warren E.
Burger, Associate Justices, William O. Douglas · William
J. Brennan, Jr. Potter Stewart · Byron White Thurgood
Marshall · Harry Blackmun Lewis F. Powell, Jr. · William
Rehnquist

John G. Roberts, Jr., Chief Justice of the United States,
Antonin Scalia, Associate Justice, Anthony M. Kennedy,

Associate Justice, Clarence Thomas, Associate Justice, Ruth Bader Ginsburg, Associate Justice, Stephen G. Breyer, Associate Justice, Samuel Anthony Alito, Jr, Associate Justice, Sonia Sotomayor, Associate Justice, Elena Kagan, Associate Justice.

We can argue the legal merits of these 3 cases from now until eternity and never settle this. I personally believe the legal merits side with the dissenters in each of the three cases. Others will disagree with me.

What I do know, beyond a shadow of a doubt is the fault lies with you and I and the rest of us Conservative Christians. We should have stood up in each case. We should have taken our responsibility to vote much more seriously.

Acts 5:29King James Version (KJV)

29 Then Peter and the other apostles answered and said, We ought to obey God rather than men.

In the Scriptures it is clear that as long as the law of the land does not contradict the law of God, we are bound to obey the law of the land. As soon as the law of the land contradicts God's command, we are to disobey the law of the land and obey God's law. This doesn't mean we are to try to over throw our Government or try to stop unjust laws with violence. We should use peaceful civil disobedience and change what we can, as soon as we can at the ballot box.

Many liberal Christians will tell you religion has no place in politics. I tell you, from a Biblical perspective that is 100% wrong. God Blessed the citizens of this great country. One of the biggest Blessing He gave us is the right to elect our leaders. That right comes with a tremendous responsibility. We have a duty not only to vote, but to research and Pray about who deserves our vote. We have a responsibility to be active and involved in choosing our leaders and to vote them out of office if they don't do what they say.

We have two quotes from Supreme Court Justices in this chapter. The first Chief Justice and the third that show how they felt. We have quotes throughout the book from signors of The Declaration of Independence and framers of our United States Constitution that prove the Warren Supreme Court of 1963 just plainly got the ruling wrong. Christians took it. We did nothing to stand up to 9 people in black robes. Now look where we are.

We can change it. We cannot undo the damage that has been done. We can't bring back the 60 million innocent children who were murdered in their Mother's womb. We can't bring back those who have lost their lives to a culture that became too permissive after prayers was taken out of schools and the public arena, but we can change it.

Oliver Ellsworth, third Chief Justice of the Supreme Court

"The primary objects of government are peace, order, and prosperity of society. To the promotion of these objects, good morals are essential. Institutions for the promotion of good morals are therefore objects of legislative provision and support, and among these, religious institutions are eminently useful and important."

A Country Divided Can Never Stand

Roger Sherman

Signer of the Declaration of Independence and United States Constitution

"I believe that there is one only living and true God, existing in three persons, the Father, the Son, and the Holy Ghost, the same in substance equal in power and glory. That the scriptures of the old and new testaments are a revelation from God, and a complete rule to direct us how we may glorify and enjoy him. That God has foreordained whatsoever comes to pass, so as thereby he is not the author or approver of sin. That he creates all things, and preserves and governs all creatures and all their actions, in a manner perfectly consistent with the freedom of will in moral agents, and the usefulness of means. That he made man at first perfectly holy, that the first man sinned, and as he was the public head of his posterity, they all became sinners in consequence of his first transgression, are wholly indisposed to that which is good and inclined to evil, and on account of sin are liable to all the miseries of this life, to death, and to the pains of hell forever.

"I believe that God having elected some of mankind to eternal life, did send his own Son to become man, die in the room and stead of sinners and thus to lay a foundation for the offer of pardon and salvation to all mankind, so as all may be saved who are willing to accept the gospel

offer: also by his special grace and spirit, to regenerate, sanctify and enable to persevere in holiness, all who shall be saved; and to procure in consequence of their repentance and faith in himself their justification by virtue of his atonement as the only meritorious cause"I believe a visible church to be a congregation of those who make a credible profession of their faith in Christ, and obedience to him, joined by the bond of the covenant.

"I believe that the souls of believers are at their death made perfectly holy, and immediately taken to glory: that at the end of this world there will be a resurrection of the dead, and a final judgement of all mankind, when the righteous shall be publicly acquitted by Christ the Judge and admitted to everlasting life and glory, and the wicked be sentenced to everlasting punishment."

--The Life of Roger Sherman, pp. 272-273.

Matthew 12:25King James Version (KJV)

25 And Jesus knew their thoughts, and said unto them, Every kingdom divided against itself is brought to desolation; and every city or house divided against itself shall not stand:

I have a fairly large front deck, I don't sleep well because of the pain from my disease. I spend a lot of hours on my deck looking up at the stars, talking to God, and praying for our country. I am very worried about the U.S. We are so divided. It breaks my heart.

Look at the comments from La Raza, from the New Black Panthers, from the Black Lives Matter's activists, from people on both ends of the political spectrum. On both ends of the abortion debate. The hate, the threats, so sad. We can disagree with each other without the threats, without the hateful rhetoric. It is horrible.

This 10 point program from the New Black Panther Party is a good example:

1. We Want Freedom. We Want Power To Determine

 The Destiny Of Our Black Community.

We believe that Black people will not be free until we are able to determine our destiny.

2. We Want Full Employment For Our People.

We believe that the federal government is responsible and obligated to give every man employment or a guaranteed income. We believe that if the White American businessmen will not give full employment, then the means of production should be taken from the businessmen and placed in the community so that the people of the community can organize and employ all of its people and give a high standard of living.

3. We Want An End To The Robbery

 By The Capitalists Of Our Black Community.

We believe that this racist government has robbed us, and now we are demanding the overdue debt of forty acres and two mules. Forty acres and two mules were promised 100 years ago as restitution for slave labor and mass murder of

Black people. We will accept the payment in currency which will be distributed to our many communities. The Germans are now aiding the Jews in Israel for the genocide of the Jewish people. The Germans murdered six million Jews. The American racist has taken part in the slaughter of over fifty million Black people; therefore, we feel that this is a modest demand that we make.

4. We Want Decent Housing Fit For The Shelter Of Human Beings.

We believe that if the White Landlords will not give decent housing to our Black community, then the housing and the land should be made into cooperatives so that our community, with government aid, can build and make decent housing for its people.

5. We Want Education For Our People That Exposes

The True Nature Of This Decadent American Society.

We Want Education That Teaches Us Our True History

And Our Role In The Present-Day Society.

We believe in an educational system that will give to our people a knowledge of self. If a man does not have knowledge of himself and his position in society and the world, then he has little chance to relate to anything else.

6. We Want All Black Men To Be Exempt From Military Service.

We believe that Black people should not be forced to fight in the military service to defend a racist government that does not protect us. We will not fight and kill other people of color in the world who, like Black people, are being victimized by the White racist government of America. We will protect ourselves from the force and violence of the racist police and the racist military, by whatever means necessary7.We Want An Immediate End To

 Police Brutality And Murder Of Black People.

We believe we can end police brutality in our Black community by organizing Black self-defense groups that are dedicated to defending our Black community from racist police oppression and brutality. The Second Amendment to the Constitution of the United States gives a right to bear arms. We therefore believe that all Black people should arm themselves for self- defense.

8.We Want Freedom For All Black Men

 Held In Federal, State, County And City Prisons And Jails.

We believe that all Black people should be released from the many jails and prisons because they have not received a fair and impartial trial.

9.We Want All Black People When Brought To Trial To Be Tried In

 Court By A Jury Of Their Peer Group Or People From Their Black

Communities, As Defined By The Constitution Of The United States.

We believe that the courts should follow the United States Constitution so that Black people will receive fair trials. The Fourteenth Amendment of the U.S. Constitution gives a man a right to be tried by his peer group. A peer is a person from a similar economic, social, religious, geographical, environmental, historical and racial background. To do this the court will be forced to select a jury from the Black community from which the Black defendant came. We have been, and are being, tried by all-White juries that have no understanding of the "average reasoning man" of the Black community.

10. We Want Land, Bread, Housing, Education,

Clothing, Justice And Peace.

When, in the course of human events, it becomes necessary for one people to dissolve the political bands which have connected them with another, and to assume, among the powers of the earth, the separate and equal station to which the laws of nature and nature's God entitle them, a decent respect of the opinions of mankind requires that they should declare the causes which impel them to the separation.

Look also at some of the statements and comments from The Black Riders Liberation Party calling for Revolution.

IT'S ON !-We need recruits everywhere, to ride on pig terrorism...

Join Now... Be A Panther At War...

For The Hearts and Minds of the People! To Be a

Member inbox or email us at blackriders1996@gmail.com- L.A. Chapter!

Black Riders - New Generation Black Panther Party for Self-Defense! RBG 4 LIFE! Black Power! All Power to the People!

PLEASE READ AND SHARE...

The Newspaper is our Number One Educational Survival Program

FROM L.A TO THE BAY, ST. LOUIS TO DETROIT, TEXAS TO NEW YORK, WE NEED A NATIONWIDE DEFENSE FORCE!

READ BLACK RIDERS NUMBER ONE RULE...

Be a Black Rider! JOIN NOW! It is time to intensify the struggle! BLACK RIDERS - new generation Black Panthers," Out of frustration and hopelessness, the Black Riders was formed by young Black people who have reached the point of no return. We refuse to be manipulated by the racist U.S. government and its ruling elite any longer into set tripping over blue and red or any "hood" or "turf" in ameriKKKa. We no longer endorse patience and turning the other cheek. We assert the right of self-defense by whatever means necessary, and reserve the right of maximum retaliation against our racist oppressors, no matter what the odds against us are.

From here on in, if we must die anyway, we will die fighting back and we will not die alone! We intend to see that our racist oppressors also get a taste of death! We will protect the Black Community with our minds, bodies, and souls. BL BLACK POWER! All Power to the People! Black Riders Number One Rule"

POINT J OUT OF OUR UPDATED 10 POINT PROGRAM CALLED THE BLACK

COMMUNE PROGRAM: WE RIDE for an immediate end to POLICE BRUTALITY and MURDER of Black People. We ride because we believe we can end police brutality in our Black community by organizing Black self-defense groups dedicated to defending our Black community from racist police oppression and brutality. The 2nd amendment of the u.s constitution gives a right to bear arms. We therefore believe that all Black people should arm themselves for self-defense.

IT IS BETTER TO DIE ON YOUR FEET THEN TO LIVE ON YOUR KNEES! IF YOU DON'T STAND FOR SOMETHING YOU'LL FALL FOR ANYTHING!

THE REVOLUTION HAS COME!

BLACK RIDERS - NEW GENERATION BLACK PANTHER PARTY FOR SELF-DEFENSE! We are now accepting Nation Wide recruits.

Inbox or email us if you are down

blackriders1996@gmail.com

YOUR PEOPLE NEED YOU... GET YOUR CITY AND STATE INVOLVED!

DON'T MISS OUT ON JOINING THE FASTEST GROWING BLACK MILITANT/

REVOLUTIONARY ORGANIZATION IN RACIST AMERIKKKA! IT IS NOW OR NEVER...

RBG 4 LIFE! ! !

PLEASE SHARE THIS WITH EVERYONE YOU KNOW!

BE A BLACK RIDER!

There's a Black Panther born in the hood every 5 minutes!

WE MUST STOP THE GENOCIDE WITH UNITY! ! !

By General T.A.C.O (Taking All capitalists Out) aka WOLVERINE SHAKUR... The Leader Of the Black Riders - NEW GENERATION BLACK PANTHER PARTY FOR SELF-DEFENSE!

"HERE'S WHAT WE DO TO UPLIFT THE BLACK COMMUNITY...We patrol the racist police with our Watch-A-Pig program, armed with video cameras and other legal weapons. We also develop survival programs because Black People are facing extermination and genocide. Some of these programs are the George Jackson Freedom School for Black Children, our Educate to Liberate Classes for Black Adults, Free Food programs for the homeless, and many, many more. Overall we push Revolution to get free from the oppressive conditions in the hood that comes from white supremacy and capitalism. Also we develop gang truces between many hoods like the Bloods and Crips in L.A to stop Black on Black violence. We push hard for Black unity! BLACK POWER! ALL POWER TO THE PEOPLE!"

(To donate by mail, you can send cash, check, or money order payable to Lakesia Wahington P.O. Box 8297 los Angeles, Ca 90008)

ENLIST NOW... TIME IS RUNNING OUT... WE MUST UNITE AND RIDE NOW!

 WE WILL NOW CRITICIZE THE UNJUST WITH THE WEAPON... BY GEORGE JACKSON - FIELD MARSHALL OF THE O. G BLACK PANTHERS! ! !

BLACK POWER! ! ! ALL POWER TO THE PEOPLE! ! ! RBG 4 LIFE!!

FROM L.A TO THE BAY, ST. LOUIS TO DETROIT, TEXAS TO NEW YORK, WE

NEED A NATIONWIDE DEFENSE FORCE!

 REST IN PEACE MIKE BROWN... EZELL FORD...
ERIC GARNER... WALTER SCOTT, FREDDIE GRAY
AND SANDRA BLAND .....REST IN POWER! ! !

The above is the absolute exact copy from their Facebook
site. This is one of their many posters:

AFRICAN INTERCOMMUNAL NEWS SERVICE

BLACK RIDERS

LIBERATION PARTY

NEW GENERATION BLACK PANTHERS

Volume 8 #1 Summer 2015 Donation $1.00

Our leaders are to be loved and admired. They will remain admired and loved no matter what the press, politicians, courts, jailers, or sell-out house negroes do or say about them. We choose and will continue to choose our leaders. Our main leader is **GENERAL T.A.C.O.**
— The Central Committee (high-ranking members) of the Black Riders - New Generation Black Panther Party for Self-Defense.

King Samir
BRLP Minister of Defense

King Samir
BRLP Minister of Defense

Watch-a-Pig! Program

The picture of General T.A.C.O. was taken in honor of Huey P. Newton during October, Black Panther History Month, although it's BPP History Month for us every month of the year. **Black Power! RGBHLife! All Power to the People!**

Watch-a-Pig! Program

Black Power March 1964 - Black Riders Matter Day - Black Riders - New Generation Black Panther Party for Self Defense - goes to Texas to March with the Huey P Newton Gun Club - **ARMED SELF-DEFENSE AGAINST THE PIGS.** General T.A.C.O. holding down the frontline, we marched on the State Capitol Building in Austin Texas, in honor of Michael Brown, Ezell Ford, Eric Garner and Clinton Allen! Black Power! All Power to the People! RBG 4 LIFE!

Another interesting tidbit from their Facebook page.

THE RACIST U.S. GOVERNMENT WAR AGAINST THE BLACK RIDERS: New Generation Black Panther Party for Self-Defense!

.

August 11, 2014 at 2:11pm

For Black youth throughout the US, especially in Watts and South Central LA, Wol...verine Shakur, AKA General T.A.C.O. of the militant Black Riders Liberation Party is a leader, a strong father and husband, a bold warrior, a ghetto hero and a down brother. Black people identify with the battle he has fought against the evil forces of white racism and reaction. They identify with this principled revolutionary struggle against the capitalist system that inevitably spells misery, suffering, and genocide for the mass of Black people held captive in Amerikkka. The Black Riders played a pivotal early part in unleashing the new wave of Black militancy that's been taking place. In 1996, General T.A.C.O. (Taking All Capitalists Out, AKA Wolverine Shakur) came together with other former Bloods and Crips in unity and created the groundwork for the resurrection of the Black Panthers, under the official name Black Riders Liberation Party. We are the new generation, and we consider ourselves to be faster, stronger, smarter and upgraded. They formulated a basic Black Commune program while in YTS prison (calling for many points as in the original 10-point program of the BPP for Self Defense, like full employment, housing, education and an end to police terrorism, and some new points, such as demanding proper medical care for AIDS victims and an immediate end to white capitalist smuggling crack cocaine into the Black community). They were eventually released to the streets and took action. Their first step was an attempt to deal with one of the most immediate and injurious symptoms of oppression – police brutality!Armed with law booklets, video cameras, camouflage fatigues and Black karate skills, bats, knives and any other legal weapons, they created the Watch-a-Pig program and began to patrol Watts and South Central L.A.'s poor Black community -- monitoring the police, observing arrests and educating brothers and sisters of their armed self-defense rights. Their determined resistance to police terrorism produced a decrease in police harassment in areas they patrolled. Panther Power to the Black Riders!

The court system in this country is increasingly becoming an important tool of repression on behalf of the exploiters. It's being used to try to crush the struggle for liberation of peace-loving poor oppressed people, not only to crush the conscious revolutionary, but to attempt to break the rebellious spirit of Black people, Chicano/Mexicanos and Puerto Ricans in general. This foul system of government is designed to oppress, exploit and intimidate all people who are not from the white Anglo-Saxon ruling class. From the violent responses of the police forces, systematic and undoubtedly calculated, it can easily be understood that the Black Riders, as opponents of this rotten system, are victims of an official conspiracy to destroy our leadership and organization. The oppressor must be harassed until his doom! He must have no peace by day or night! Free all political prisoners of war! When the prison doors are opened, the true dragon will fly out!

BLACK POWER! ! ! ALL POWER TO THE PEOPLE! !

Louis Farrakhan, the leader of the Nation of Islam, another divider recently said this at a Church in Miami, Fl:

"And the police when they kill us, they put the lie out first and then back the lie up with the institutions of government of White Supremacy. And so even though we march and even though we fight against this injustice it continues unabated. So we have decided on the 20th anniversary of the Million Man March we want to go to Washington.

"We want to go back to Washington to demand of our government what we rightly deserve and what we have paid for with our sweat and our blood," the Minister declared. "But this time we are not asking for justice, we are demanding justice and as Frederick Douglass says, 'power concedes nothing without a demand.' And I added to that, power concedes nothing without a demand that is backed by power."

"So what is the power that should back our righteous demand for justice? It is the unequaled power of our unity as a people. We have never 'gone united.' We stay as little tribes and factions, gathering only for the moment and then scattering after the moment. But when you and I can go as a people, not Muslim and Christian and Baptists, and Methodists, and Crips and Bloods, and native tribes, but go as the original inhabitants of our planet to demand justice and some of this earth we can call our own," he said.

Between men and women there is a demand from nature that must be satisfied to bring unity and harmony, the Minister said. The man must give first as the maintainer, the protector, the provider for the woman in his life and the woman will respond to an unspoken demand out of the beauty of her nature, he said. But, the Minister noted, Satan has turned things upside down with women working, factories closed, and Blacks left in the lurch, unable to create jobs and unwilling to support Black entrepreneurs. And Blacks bereft of the knowledge of self beg others to do what Blacks must do for themselves, he continued. Those who provide goods and services take money out of an underdeveloped and disrespected community without substantial reinvestment.

Such social engineering leaves Uncle Sam ready to recruit fearless Black youth in the armed forces, and the U.S. government helped foment the crack cocaine epidemic by placing drugs and weapons in the 'hood to promote fratricide and Black discord, he said. The wise of this nation, and leaders like J. Edgar Hoover, the longtime FBI director, know it is time for the rise of Black people and are determined to avert the destruction and fall of White supremacy, the Minister noted.

But like a serpent, Whites are deceptive, trying to keep control of the once-slaves who are destined to go free by monitoring their activities, their leaders, their actions and even their social media posts to cull information, he said.

"They would like to charge us with radicalizing our people by telling the truth, but every time they kill a Black man or beat up a Black woman or unjustly stop us for traffic violation and then kill us, we are being radicalized. They are the ones who are radicalizing us. All we are doing is telling the truth of what they are doing,"

Later in his message, the Minister called for 10,000 fearless men willing to make the ultimate sacrifice rather than live under tyranny. There comes a time in the life of every people who yearn for freedom where death is sweeter than to continue life under oppression, he said. Blacks must protect their lives if the federal government refuses to intervene when Black lives are unjustly and the principle of a life of a life is laid out in scripture, the Minister explained. "Death is sweeter than to continue to live and bury our children while White folks give the killers hamburgers. Death is sweeter than watching us slaughter each other to the joy of a 400-year-old enemy. Death is sweeter. The Qur'an teaches persecution is worse than slaughter then it says, retaliation is prescribed in matters of the slain. Retaliation is a prescription from God to calm the breasts of those whose children have been slain. If the federal government will not intercede in our affairs, then we must rise up and kill those who kill us, stalk them and let them feel the pain of death that we are feeling."

It isn't only a few radical Black groups who are attempting to divide us or call for armed rebellion, unfortunately there doesn't seem to be any one race or culture that is the only one. This divisiveness and hatred seems to come from the far right or far left of every race, religion, or culture in America. The next one listed is called The Plan. It is advocated by both La Raza and MEChA.

Movimiento Estudiantil Chicano de Aztlán (MEChA) is a student organization that promotes higher education, cultura, and historia. MEChA was founded on the principles of self-determination for the liberation of our people. We believe that political involvement and education is the avenue for change in our society.

Each word in MEChA symbolizes a great concept in terms of la causa. Movimiento means that the organization is dedicated to the movement to gain self-determination for our people. Estudiantil, identifies the organization as a student group for we are part of our Raza's future. At the heart of the name is the use of the identity: Chicano. At first seen as a negative word, now taken for a badge of honor. In adopting their new identity, the students committed themselves to return to the barrios, colonias, or campos and together, struggle against the forces that oppress our gente. Lastly, the affirmation that we are Indigenous people to this land by placing our movement in Aztlan, the homeland of all peoples from Anahuak.

On campuses across Aztlan, MEChA and Mechistas are often the only groups on campus Raza and non-Raza alike that seek to open the doors of higher education para nuestras comunidades and strive for a society free of imperialism, racism, sexism, and homophobia. An inspirational statement in El Plan Santa Barbara that speaks to this notes:

"MEChA must bring to the mind of every young Chicana and Chicano that the liberation of her/his people from prejudice and oppression is in her/his hands and this responsibility is greater than personal achievement and more meaningful than degrees, especially if they are earned at the expense of her/his identity and cultural integrity. MEChA, then, is more than a name; it is a spirit of unity, of sisterhood and brotherhood, and a resolve to undertake a struggle for liberation in society where justice is but a word. MEChA is a means to an end" (El Plan de Santa Barbara).

El Plan de Aztlan (El Plan Espiritual de Aztlan)

In the spirit of a new people that is conscious not only of its proud historical heritage but also of the brutal "gringo" invasion of our territories, we, the Chicano inhabitants and civilizers of the northern land of Aztlan from whence came our forefathers, reclaiming the land of their birth and consecrating the determination of our people of the sun, declare that the call of our blood is our power, our responsibility, and our inevitable destiny.

We are free and sovereign to determine those tasks which are justly called for by our house, our land, the sweat of our brows, and by our hearts. Aztlan belongs to those who plant the seeds, water the fields, and gather the crops and not to the foreign Europeans. We do not recognize capricious frontiers on the bronze continent.

Brotherhood unites us, and love for our brothers makes us a people whose time has come and who struggles against the foreigner "gabacho" who exploits our riches and destroys our culture. With our heart in our hands and our hands in the soil, we declare the independence of our mestizo nation. We are a bronze people with a bronze culture. Before the world, before all of North America, before all our brothers in the bronze continent, we are a nation, we are a union of free pueblos, we are Aztlan.

Program

El Plan Espiritual de Aztlan sets the theme that the Chicanos (La Raza de Bronze) must use their nationalism as the key or common denominator for mass mobilization and organization. Once we are committed to the idea and philosophy of El Plan de Aztlan, we can only conclude that social, economic, cultural, and political independence is the only road to total liberation from oppression, exploitation, and racism. Our struggle then must be for the control of our barrios, campos, pueblos, lands, our economy, our culture, and our political life. El Plan commits all levels of Chicano society--the barrio, the campo, the ranchero, the writer, the teacher, the worker, the professional--to La Causa.Nationalism

Nationalism as the key to organization transcends all religious, political, class, and economic factions or boundaries. Nationalism is the common denominator that all members of La Raza can agree upon.

Organizational Goals

1. UNITY in the thinking of our people concerning the barrios, the pueblo, the campo, the land, the poor, the middle class, the professional--all committed to the liberation of La Raza.

2. ECONOMY: economic control of our lives and our communities can only come about by driving the exploiter out of our communities, our pueblos, and our lands and by controlling and developing our own talents, sweat, and resources. Cultural background and values which ignore materialism and embrace humanism will contribute to the act of cooperative buying and the distribution of resources and production to sustain an economic base for healthy growth and development Lands rightfully ours will be fought for and defended. Land and realty ownership will be acquired by the community for the people's welfare. Economic ties of responsibility must be secured by nationalism and the Chicano defense units.

3. EDUCATION must be relative to our people, i.e., history, culture, bilingual education, contributions, etc. Community control of our schools, our teachers, our administrators, our counselors, and our programs.

4. INSTITUTIONS shall serve our people by providing the service necessary for a full life and their welfare on the basis of restitution, not handouts or beggar's crumbs. Restitution for past economic slavery, political

exploitation, ethnic and cultural psychological destruction and denial of civil and human rights. Institutions in our community which do not serve the people have no place in the community. The institutions belong to the people.

5. SELF-DEFENSE of the community must rely on the combined strength of the people. The front line defense will come from the barrios, the campos, the pueblos, and the ranchitos. Their involvement as protectors of their people will be given respect and dignity. They in turn offer their responsibility and their lives for their people. Those who place themselves in the front ranks for their people do so out of love and carnalismo. Those institutions which are fattened by our brothers to provide employment and political pork barrels for the gringo will do so only as acts of liberation and for La Causa. For the very young there will no longer be acts of juvenile delinquency, but revolutionary acts.6. CULTURAL values of our people strengthen our identity and the moral backbone of the movement. Our culture unites and educates the family of La Raza towards liberation with one heart and one mind. We must insure that our writers, poets, musicians, and artists produce literature and art that is appealing to our people and relates to our revolutionary culture. Our cultural values of life, family, and home will serve as a powerful weapon to defeat the gringo dollar value system and encourage the process of love and brotherhood.

7. POLITICAL LIBERATION can only come through independent action on our part, since the two-party system is the same animal with two heads that feed from the same trough. Where we are a majority, we will control; where

we are a minority, we will represent a pressure group; nationally, we will represent one party: La Familia de La Raza!

Action

1. Awareness and distribution of El Plan Espiritual de Aztlan. Presented at every meeting, demonstration, confrontation, courthouse, institution, administration, church, school, tree, building, car, and every place of human existence.

2. September 16, on the birth date of Mexican Independence, a national walk-out by all Chicanos of all colleges and schools to be sustained until the complete revision of the educational system: its policy makers, administration, its curriculum, and its personnel to meet the needs of our community.

3. Self-Defense against the occupying forces of the oppressors at every school, every available man, woman, and child.

4. Community nationalization and organization of all Chicanos: El Plan Espiritual de Aztlan.

5. Economic program to drive the exploiter out of our community and a welding together of our people's combined resources to control their own production through cooperative effort.

6. Creation of an independent local, regional, and national political party. A nation autonomous and free--culturally, socially, economically, and politically--will make its own

decisions on the usage of our lands, the taxation of our goods, the utilization of our bodies for war, the determination of justice (reward and punishment), and the profit of our sweat.

El Plan de Aztlan is the plan of liberation!

Make no mistake, this is not just a black or Hispanic or liberal problem. I only highlighted these groups because their internet posts, their blogs, and their internet radio programs show what I believe is a federal crime. Read the statute and see what you think.

18 U.S. Code § 2385 - Advocating overthrow of Government

Whoever knowingly or willfully advocates, abets, advises, or teaches the duty, necessity, desirability, or propriety of overthrowing or destroying the government of the United States or the government of any State, Territory, District or Possession thereof, or the government of any political subdivision therein, by force or violence, or by the assassination of any officer of any such government; or

Whoever, with intent to cause the overthrow or destruction of any such government, prints, publishes, edits, issues, circulates, sells, distributes, or publicly displays any written or printed matter advocating, advising, or teaching the duty, necessity, desirability, or propriety of overthrowing or destroying any government in the United States by force or violence, or attempts to do so; or

Whoever organizes or helps or attempts to organize any society, group, or assembly of persons who teach, advocate, or encourage the overthrow or destruction of any such government by force or violence; or becomes or is a member of, or affiliates with, any such society, group, or assembly of persons, knowing the purposes thereof—

Shall be fined under this title or imprisoned not more than twenty years, or both, and shall be ineligible for employment by the United States or any department or agency thereof, for the five years next following his conviction.

If two or more persons conspire to commit any offense named in this section, each shall be fined under this title or imprisoned not more than twenty years, or both, and shall be ineligible for employment by the United States or any department or agency thereof, for the five years next following his conviction.

As used in this section, the terms "organizes" and "organize", with respect to any society, group, or assembly of persons, include the recruiting of new members, the forming of new units, and the regrouping or expansion of existing clubs, classes, and other units of such society, group, or assembly of persons.

18 U.S. Code § 2384 - Seditious conspiracy

If two or more persons in any State or Territory, or in any place subject to the jurisdiction of the United States, conspire to overthrow, put down, or to destroy by force the Government of the United States, or to levy war against them, or to oppose by force the authority thereof, or by force to prevent, hinder, or delay the execution of any law of the United States, or by force to seize, take, or possess any property of the United States contrary to the authority thereof, they shall each be fined under this title or imprisoned not more than twenty years, or both.

The way I read the statute every one of the groups listed above should be charged under one or both of these statutes.

All you have to do is go to social media sites such as Facebook or twitter type in #PlannedParenthood and read the comments. You will see so much hate and divisiveness it will make you sick. From both sides of the abortion argument. Read the articles from news services on Planned Parenthood, then go beneath the article and read the comments. That we as a country can't come together and agree that murdering babies and selling the body parts is not wrong shows just how divided we are. Very sad.

Type in Israel or Palestine and read the comments. My goodness, the hate spouted on those sites is unbelievable, and very, very sad.

Then there are the White Supremacist groups, the KKK, the Skinheads, some of the Militia Groups. Muslim groups advocating replacing our Constitution with Sharia. The drug gangs, many of them plot to overthrow the government. The list goes on and on. Al Sharpton, Jesse Jackson, and others like them of all races have made a very nice living sowing seeds of hatred and division.

The question becomes how did we get in this place and how do we get out of it? Obviously as a Preacher I say Satan is how we got in this place, and Prayer and God is how we get out.

As a citizen of this country I say that, but I think there are things we can and should be willing to admit and do something about. That is really what this entire book is about. Had we as a nation not turned our back on God much of this would not be happening. The breakdown of the family is a huge part of it. Parents trying to be friends with their children instead of being a parent and teaching discipline. The failed Democratic policies in the "War on Poverty" programs are part of it.

Preachers not preaching the full Word of God in our Churches is a very large part of it.

In my heart I believe if we could all begin to come together and follow the Biblical principles God gave us, He would help us turn this country around quickly. Will it be easy? No. Will it be painful? Yes. We will be disciplined as a nation for turning our backs on him. Will it be worth it? Absolutely!!

Please join me in Praying this Prayer or one like it as often as you can. We need it. Our country needs it. Jean, my lovely wife and I Pray for America together. At least 3 times a day we do. Will you join us?

A Prayer for America

O Lord, I thank you for allowing me to be born in this great land. Our Nation is hurting right now God as you know. We need you now as much or more than any time in our history.

God I know many of our pains are self-inflicted. As a country we have turned our backs on you. We have allowed Satan to divide us, we have allowed success to make us feel entitled. We have taken so much for granted. We are in more trouble than ever.

I know Dear God when you look at us you must weep in sadness over what we have done to this country you blessed us with. Over how many of us have turned our back on you.

O Lord as you know we still have some Righteous people in this great land. I pray God you use us to help spark a Great Revival in our country. I pray you help us turn this country back to you! On my knees I beg you to heal our land! Bring us together! Heal our divides! Turn our hearts and our eyes back toward you!

Dear God I want so to leave my children, my grandchildren and those that come behind a better America. A better world. We can't do that without you

God. Our external enemies are circling. They see how divided we are. They know when we are divided we are weak, and they are ready to attack. Satan is happy. I know if we humble ourselves to you and look to you once again you will bless our country.

I thank you God for this group of Prayer Warriors. I thank you for hearing our Prayers. I thank you for all the Blessings we take for granted. Please heal our land!

In Jesus name I Pray. Amen.

Chapter 7 - What We Should Do With Our Old Churches

Benjamin Rush

Signer of the Declaration of Independence and Ratifier of the U.S. Constitution

"The gospel of Jesus Christ prescribes the wisest rules for just conduct in every situation of life. Happy they who are enabled to obey them in all situations!"

--The Autobiography of Benjamin Rush, pp. 165-166.

"Christianity is the only true and perfect religion, and that in proportion as mankind adopts its principles and obeys its precepts, they will be wise and happy."

"I know there is an objection among many people to teaching children doctrines of any kind, because they are liable to be controverted. But let us not be wiser than our Maker.

"If moral precepts alone could have reformed mankind, the mission of the Son of God into all the world would have been unnecessary. The perfect morality of the gospel rests upon the doctrine which, though often controverted has never been refuted: I mean the vicarious life and death of the Son of God."

--Essays, Literary, Moral, and Philosophical, published in 1798

I have watched heartbroken as Church after Church in the community I grew up in has either closed or relocated out of the community. I am a firm believer when a Church moves out of a community it leaves a Spiritual vacuum in that community. Anytime there is a Spiritual vacuum you can bet Satan will fill it. We shouldn't close it we should change it!

As once middle class neighborhoods slide into poverty, and middle class families move out, we see Churches lose attendance. Lose membership, and lose donations. Then we see the Churches both move out and close their physical building, putting it up for sale or lease. Sometimes they may keep it open but just scale back to serve the older people that did not or could not move out of the community.

I strongly feel when we do that we are surrendering that community to Satan. Why not treat the old Church as a way to reach people you ordinarily may not be able to reach? Isn't that what we a really commanded to do in the Bible?

Many of these Churches have excellent buildings that could be used to really help change the entire community. We know from history when Churches become the center of a neighborhood or community, the community flourishes.

You would need Church leaders and volunteers that were 100% committed but think of the rewards! This is what the Lord spoke too my heart about. Find an old Church property that has a kitchen, preferably a gym, a daycare center, a fellowship hall and plenty of class rooms. Then the hard but rewarding work begins.

Write out a plan. I am going to share the ideas I was given with you. If my health was in better shape I would have started this 6 years ago when God first put it on my heart. Of course had I obeyed, my health may be better by now!

My plan would include but not be limited to:

1. Start a food pantry.
2. Set up a thrift store on the premises. Every item $1.00. The idea is not to make money but help individuals and families who need it the most.
3. Set up a daycare for working families. The charge would be based on the parent or parents' ability to pay. Many would get this service free of charge.
4. Find current and retired Teachers to tutor students who need or desire a tutor. No charge.
5. Find current and retired students to teach classes to prepare for the GED Exam, as well as ACT and SAT exams.
6. Use one room for a computer lab to teach computer programing and repair.
7. Use the kitchen to prepare lunch for senior citizens Monday thru Friday. A safe haven where they can get out of their house and have at least one hot nourishing meal a day. A place they can be among people instead of sitting home alone.
8. Invite and encourage men and women of faith who were able with God's help to overcome poverty to share their Testimony.

9. Pay teens who have no other way of making money to go out with volunteers from the Church to the homes of senior citizens and the disabled to do yard work and other things they aren't able to do themselves.
10. Try to find volunteers who are certified plumbers, electricians, HVAC repair, carpenters, mechanics, welders, and health care workers to come teach classes to young adults to help them get into a career, trade school or college.
11. Have an adult English language class to help immigrants assimilate.
12. Have activities with security in the gym afternoons and evenings to give young people a safe environment to participate in sports, music, arts and crafts etc…
13. Search the thrift stores and seek donations for musical instruments. Try to find a retired or current band teacher to teach music classes to children.
14. Recruit a retired or current drama teacher to start a drama club.
15. Recruit local business leaders to start job training programs. To come in and teach interview skills. To explain what they look for in an employee. To start mentoring programs.
16. Recruit volunteers to go door to door in the community inviting people to Church. Have them pray with the people they visit. Explain the Church programs and Mission Statement. Encourage them to sit a table up at local stores, strip centers, etc… and pass out literature about the Church and Church

programs. Pray with anyone who will let them. Encourage them to come Worship with the Church.

17. Try to have community events at the Church one Saturday a month. You could have local college sports teams come sign autographs. Invite Choirs from different Churches to come and put on free concerts. Use your imagination. Anything that does not go against Scripture to build excitement and positive energy. Anything that would be pleasing to God.

18. Have Christian based Family Counseling, Marital Counseling. Have a training program for expectant Mothers. Give them a Christ centered alternative to Planned Parenthood.

19. Most importantly preach the Word of God. All of it. Not just the feel good parts. Pray for the community. Establish prayer groups that will be committed to pray for the community and the Church daily.

Obviously this would be a massive undertaking. It would require a tremendous amount of commitment. A tremendous amount of fundraising. A lot of patience and prayer. I feel in my heart and soul it would be worth every bit of it.

With God's help and blessings you could be a part of something great. The Church would be doing exactly what God commanded. Feeding the poor. Giving them a hand up. Sharing the Word of God with them. Helping prepare them for the future. Helping restore hope.

Losing hope is a terrible thing. Probably second only to losing your Salvation. I guess in a way losing hope is losing Salvation. Losing hope when you get right to it is losing faith that God will get you thru the difficult times.

Many of the people in these communities have lost hope. How much more noble of a cause can you find than helping restore hope? Than helping share the word and the love of our Lord and Savior? Than offering people not just a handout but a hand up.

Chapter 8 Barack H. Obama

John Adams

2nd U.S. President and Signer of the Declaration of Independence

"Suppose a nation in some distant Region should take the Bible for their only law Book, and every member should regulate his conduct by the precepts there exhibited! Every member would be obliged in conscience, to temperance, frugality, and industry; to justice, kindness, and charity towards his fellow men; and to piety, love, and reverence toward Almighty God ... What a Eutopia, what a Paradise would this region be."

President Obama is the most divisive, anti-Christian, anti-Israel President in the history of the United States of America.

First lets look at his stated views on Christianity.

1. "Whatever we once were, we are no longer a Christian nation"

The large majority of Americans -- 77% of the adult population -- identify with a Christian religion, including

52% who are Protestants or some other non-Catholic Christian religion, 23% who are Catholic, and 2% who affiliate with the Church of Jesus Christ of Latter-day Saints. Another 18% of Americans do not have an explicit religious identity and 5% identify with a non-Christian religion.

The Scriptures say:

The Scriptures say:

Isaiah 1:4New International Version (NIV)

4 Woe to the sinful nation, a people whose guilt is great, a brood of evildoers, children given to corruption! They have forsaken the Lord; they have spurned the Holy One of Israel and turned their backs on Him.

2. "Which passages of scripture should guide our public policy? Should we go with Leviticus, which suggests slavery is OK and that eating shellfish is an abomination? Or we could go with Deuteronomy, which suggests stoning your child if he strays from the faith?"

3. "Even those who claim the Bible's inerrancy make distinctions between Scriptural edicts, sensing that some passages – the Ten Commandments, say, or a belief in Christ's divinity – are central to Christian faith, while others are more culturally specific and may be modified to accommodate modern life."

Answer to 2 & 3:

The teachings of Jesus, the Council of Jerusalem, and other New Testament teachings (John 1:16-17, Acts 13:39, Romans 2:25-29, 8:1-4, 1 Corinthians 9:19-21, Galatians 2:15-16, Ephesians 2:15) make it clear that Christians are not required to follow the Old Testament rules about crimes and punishments, warfare, slavery, diet, circumcision, animal sacrifices, feast days, Sabbath observance, ritual cleanness, etc.

Christians still look to the Old Testament scripture for moral and spiritual guidance (2 Timothy 3:16-17). But when there seems to be a conflict between Old Testament laws and New Testament principles, we must follow the New Testament because it represents the most recent and most perfect revelation from God (Hebrews 8:13, 2 Corinthians 3:1-18, Galatians 2:15-20).

However, freedom from the Old Testament Law is not a license for Christians to relax their moral standards. The moral and ethical teachings of Jesus and His apostles call for even greater self-discipline than those of the Old Testament (Matthew 5:21-22, 27-28, 31-32, 33-34, 38-42, 43-48, 7:1-5, 15:18-19, 25:37-40, Mark 7:21-23, 12:28-31, Luke 12:15, 1 Corinthians 13:1-13, Galatians 5:19-21, James 1:27, 2:15-16, 1 John 3:17-19).

4. "The American people intuitively understand this, which is why the majority of Catholics practice birth

control and some of those opposed to gay marriage nevertheless are opposed to a Constitutional amendment to ban it. Religious leadership need not accept such wisdom in counseling their flocks, but they should recognize this wisdom in their politics."

"Religious leadership need not accept such wisdom in counseling their flocks, but they should recognize this wisdom in their politics". WHAT? Barack H. Obama does not tell me what to Preach. The Holy Spirit and The Holy Scriptures do. Many of BHO's policies are totally inconsistent with Biblical teachings. What he is saying is its ok for me to Preach the Bible in the Church but separate my Religious beliefs, the core of who I am so I can agree with him politically. Has some one made him The Messiah? I think not.

5. From Obama's book, The Audacity of Hope: "I am not willing to have the state deny American citizens a civil union that confers equivalent rights on such basic matters as hospital visitation or health insurance coverage simply because the people they love are of the same sex—nor am I willing to accept a reading of the Bible that considers an obscure line in Romans to be more defining of Christianity than the Sermon on the Mount."

I hate to tell President Obama, but there is no "obscure line" in the Holy Bible. They are all important. That "obscure line in Romans" is not the only place in The Holy Scriptures that discuss Homosexuality.

Here is President Obama's "obscure line":

Romans 1:18-32 King James Version (KJV)

18 For the wrath of God is revealed from heaven against all ungodliness and unrighteousness of men, who hold the truth in unrighteousness;

19 Because that which may be known of God is manifest in them; for God hath shewed it unto them.

20 For the invisible things of him from the creation of the world are clearly seen, being understood by the things that are made, even his eternal power and Godhead; so that they are without excuse:

21 Because that, when they knew God, they glorified him not as God, neither were thankful; but became vain in their imaginations, and their foolish heart was darkened.

22 Professing themselves to be wise, they became fools,

23 And changed the glory of the uncorruptible God into an image made like to corruptible man, and to birds, and fourfooted beasts, and creeping things.

24 Wherefore God also gave them up to uncleanness through the lusts of their own hearts, to dishonour their own bodies between themselves:

25 Who changed the truth of God into a lie, and worshipped and served the creature more than the Creator, who is blessed for ever. Amen.

26 For this cause God gave them up unto vile affections: for even their women did change the natural use into that which is against nature:

27 And likewise also the men, leaving the natural use of the woman, burned in their lust one toward another; men with men working that which is unseemly, and receiving in themselves that recompence of their error which was meet.

28 And even as they did not like to retain God in their knowledge, God gave them over to a reprobate mind, to do those things which are not convenient;

29 Being filled with all unrighteousness, fornication, wickedness, covetousness, maliciousness; full of envy, murder, debate, deceit, malignity; whisperers,

30 Backbiters, haters of God, despiteful, proud, boasters, inventors of evil things, disobedient to parents,

31 Without understanding, covenantbreakers, without natural affection, implacable, unmerciful:

32 Who knowing the judgment of God, that they which commit such things are worthy of death, not only do the same, but have pleasure in them that do them.

That is a little more than an "obscure line" President Obama. In addition there is this:

Mark 7:20-23King James Version (KJV)

20 And he said, That which cometh out of the man, that defileth the man.

21 For from within, out of the heart of men, proceed evil thoughts, adulteries, fornications, murders,

22 Thefts, covetousness, wickedness, deceit, lasciviousness, an evil eye, blasphemy, pride, foolishness:

23 All these evil things come from within, and defile the man

1 Corinthians 6:9-10New International Version (NIV)

9 Or do you not know that wrongdoers will not inherit the kingdom of God? Do not be deceived: Neither the sexually immoral nor idolaters nor adulterers nor men who have sex with men[a] 10 nor thieves nor the greedy nor drunkards nor slanderers nor swindlers will inherit the kingdom of God.

1 Timothy 1:8-11New International Version (NIV)

8 We know that the law is good if one uses it properly. 9 We also know that the law is made not for the righteous but for lawbreakers and rebels, the ungodly and sinful, the unholy and irreligious, for those who kill their fathers or mothers, for murderers, 10 for the sexually immoral, for those practicing homosexuality, for slave traders and liars and perjurers—and for whatever else is contrary to the sound doctrine 11 that conforms to the gospel concerning the glory of the blessed God, which he entrusted to me.

Genesis 19:1-13King James Version (KJV)

1 And there came two angels to Sodom at even; and Lot sat in the gate of Sodom: and Lot seeing them rose up to

meet them; and he bowed himself with his face toward the ground;

2 And he said, Behold now, my lords, turn in, I pray you, into your servant's house, and tarry all night, and wash your feet, and ye shall rise up early, and go on your ways. And they said, Nay; but we will abide in the street all night.

3 And he pressed upon them greatly; and they turned in unto him, and entered into his house; and he made them a feast, and did bake unleavened bread, and they did eat.

4 But before they lay down, the men of the city, even the men of Sodom, compassed the house round, both old and young, all the people from every quarter:

5 And they called unto Lot, and said unto him, Where are the men which came in to thee this night? bring them out unto us, that we may know them.

6 And Lot went out at the door unto them, and shut the door after him,

7 And said, I pray you, brethren, do not so wickedly.

8 Behold now, I have two daughters which have not known man; let me, I pray you, bring them out unto you, and do ye to them as is good in your eyes: only unto these men do nothing; for therefore came they under the shadow of my roof.

9 And they said, Stand back. And they said again, This one fellow came in to sojourn, and he will needs be a judge: now will we deal worse with thee, than with them. And

they pressed sore upon the man, even Lot, and came near to break the door.

10 But the men put forth their hand, and pulled Lot into the house to them, and shut to the door.

11 And they smote the men that were at the door of the house with blindness, both small and great: so that they wearied themselves to find the door.

12 And the men said unto Lot, Hast thou here any besides? son in law, and thy sons, and thy daughters, and whatsoever thou hast in the city, bring them out of this place:

13 For we will destroy this place, because the cry of them is waxen great before the face of the Lord; and the Lord hath sent us to destroy it.

Leviticus 18:21-22New International Version (NIV)

21 "'Do not give any of your children to be sacrificed to Molek, for you must not profane the name of your God. I am the Lord.

22 "'Do not have sexual relations with a man as one does with a woman; that is detestable.

Leviticus 20:13New International Version (NIV)

13 "'If a man has sexual relations with a man as one does with a woman, both of them have done what is detestable. They are to be put to death; their blood will be on their own heads.

Judges 19:20-23New International Version (NIV)

20 "You are welcome at my house," the old man said. "Let me supply whatever you need. Only don't spend the night in the square." 21 So he took him into his house and fed his donkeys. After they had washed their feet, they had something to eat and drink.

22 While they were enjoying themselves, some of the wicked men of the city surrounded the house. Pounding on the door, they shouted to the old man who owned the house, "Bring out the man who came to your house so we can have sex with him."

23 The owner of the house went outside and said to them, "No, my friends, don't be so vile. Since this man is my guest, don't do this outrageous thing.

As anyone can see President Obama, it is far more than "one obscure line in Romans."

   6. Obama's response when asked what his definition of sin is: "Being out of alignment with my values."

This really doesn't even deserve a response. This is President Obama acting as if he knows more than Jesus Christ. President Obama, The Bible is not like an all you can eat Buffet, you can't just take what you want and leave the rest.

1 John 5:17King James Version (KJV)

17 All unrighteousness is sin: and there is a sin not unto death.

Matthew 12:31King James Version (KJV)

31 Wherefore I say unto you, All manner of sin and blasphemy shall be forgiven unto men: but the blasphemy against the Holy Ghost shall not be forgiven unto men.

Mark 1:4King James Version (KJV)

4 John did baptize in the wilderness, and preach the baptism of repentance for the remission of sins.

Mark 8:38King James Version (KJV)

38 Whosoever therefore shall be ashamed of me and of my words in this adulterous and sinful generation; of him also shall the Son of man be ashamed, when he cometh in the glory of his Father with the holy angels.

1 John 3:8King James Version (KJV)

8 He that committeth sin is of the devil; for the devil sinneth from the beginning. For this purpose the Son of God was manifested, that he might destroy the works of the devil.

7. "If all it took was someone proclaiming I believe Jesus Christ and that he died for my sins, and that was all there was to it, people wouldn't have to keep coming to church, would they."

Again, he is wrong and tries to over simplify things. First of all nowhere does it say if you are proclaim Jesus Christ is Lord and He died for my sins, you do or do not have to go to Church. What The Bible teaches us is if you are truly Saved, if you've truly been washed in the Blood of Jesus you will want to be away from sin and sinful temptations. You will want to be around other Born Again Christians. You will want to Serve God. You will want to go Worship God with other Believers.

As James said:

James 2:14-26King James Version (KJV)

14 What doth it profit, my brethren, though a man say he hath faith, and have not works? can faith save him?

15 If a brother or sister be naked, and destitute of daily food,

16 And one of you say unto them, Depart in peace, be ye warmed and filled; notwithstanding ye give them not those things which are needful to the body; what doth it profit?

17 Even so faith, if it hath not works, is dead, being alone.

18 Yea, a man may say, Thou hast faith, and I have works: shew me thy faith without thy works, and I will shew thee my faith by my works.

19 Thou believest that there is one God; thou doest well: the devils also believe, and tremble.

20 But wilt thou know, O vain man, that faith without works is dead?

21 Was not Abraham our father justified by works, when he had offered Isaac his son upon the altar?

22 Seest thou how faith wrought with his works, and by works was faith made perfect?

23 And the scripture was fulfilled which saith, Abraham believed God, and it was imputed unto him for righteousness: and he was called the Friend of God.

24 Ye see then how that by works a man is justified, and not by faith only.

25 Likewise also was not Rahab the harlot justified by works, when she had received the messengers, and had sent them out another way?

26 For as the body without the spirit is dead, so faith without works is dead also.

8. "This is something that I'm sure I'd have serious debates with my fellow Christians about. I think that the difficult thing about any religion, including Christianity, is that at some level there is a call to evangelize and prostelytize. There's the belief, certainly in some quarters, that people haven't embraced Jesus Christ as their personal savior that they're going to hell."

This one is almost too easy. The hardest part is picking out which Scripture out of the multitude which refute President Obama's comment.

John 14:1-21 King James Version (KJV)

14 Let not your heart be troubled: ye believe in God, believe also in me.

2 In my Father's house are many mansions: if it were not so, I would have told you. I go to prepare a place for you.

3 And if I go and prepare a place for you, I will come again, and receive you unto myself; that where I am, there ye may be also.

4 And whither I go ye know, and the way ye know.

5 Thomas saith unto him, Lord, we know not whither thou goest; and how can we know the way?

6 Jesus saith unto him, I am the way, the truth, and the life: no man cometh unto the Father, but by me.

7 If ye had known me, ye should have known my Father also: and from henceforth ye know him, and have seen him.

8 Philip saith unto him, Lord, show us the Father, and it sufficeth us.

9 Jesus saith unto him, Have I been so long time with you, and yet hast thou not known me, Philip? he that hath seen me hath seen the Father; and how sayest thou then, Show us the Father?

10 Believest thou not that I am in the Father, and the Father in me? the words that I speak unto you I speak not of myself: but the Father that dwelleth in me, he doeth the works.

11 Believe me that I am in the Father, and the Father in me: or else believe me for the very works' sake.

12 Verily, verily, I say unto you, He that believeth on me, the works that I do shall he do also; and greater works than these shall he do; because I go unto my Father.

13 And whatsoever ye shall ask in my name, that will I do, that the Father may be glorified in the Son.

14 If ye shall ask any thing in my name, I will do it.

15 If ye love me, keep my commandments.

16 And I will pray the Father, and he shall give you another Comforter, that he may abide with you for ever;

17 Even the Spirit of truth; whom the world cannot receive, because it seeth him not, neither knoweth him: but ye know him; for he dwelleth with you, and shall be in you.

18 I will not leave you comfortless: I will come to you.

19 Yet a little while, and the world seeth me no more; but ye see me: because I live, ye shall live also.

20 At that day ye shall know that I am in my Father, and ye in me, and I in you.

21 He that hath my commandments, and keepeth them, he it is that loveth me: and he that loveth me shall be loved of my Father, and I will love him, and will manifest myself to him.

9. "I find it hard to believe that my God would consign four-fifths of the world to hell. I can't imagine that my God would allow some little Hindu kid in India who never interacts with the Christian faith to somehow burn for all eternity. That's just not part of my religious makeup."

I have to be careful here. These few statements are so similar and there is so much Scripture I could use to refute the statements it would seem as if all I did was reprint the Bible. I will try to use only enough to show how ridiculous his statements are.

Leviticus 5:17King James Version (KJV)

17 And if a soul sin, and commit any of these things which are forbidden to be done by the commandments of the Lord; though he wist it not, yet is he guilty, and shall bear his iniquity.

10. "I don't presume to have knowledge of what happens after I die. But I feel very strongly that whether the reward is in the here and now or in the hereafter, the aligning myself to my faith and my values is a good thing."

Matthew 7:13-20King James Version (KJV)

13 Enter ye in at the strait gate: for wide is the gate, and broad is the way, that leadeth to destruction, and many there be which go in thereat:

14 Because strait is the gate, and narrow is the way, which leadeth unto life, and few there be that find it.

15 Beware of false prophets, which come to you in sheep's clothing, but inwardly they are ravening wolves.

16 Ye shall know them by their fruits. Do men gather grapes of thorns, or figs of thistles?

17 Even so every good tree bringeth forth good fruit; but a corrupt tree bringeth forth evil fruit.

18 A good tree cannot bring forth evil fruit, neither can a corrupt tree bring forth good fruit.

19 Every tree that bringeth not forth good fruit is hewn down, and cast into the fire.

20 Wherefore by their fruits ye shall know them.

11. "I've said this before, and I know this raises questions in the minds of some evangelicals. I do not believe that my mother, who never formally embraced Christianity as far as I know … I do not believe she went to hell."

Matthew 7:21-23King James Version (KJV)

21 Not every one that saith unto me, Lord, Lord, shall enter into the kingdom of heaven; but he that doeth the will of my Father which is in heaven.

22 Many will say to me in that day, Lord, Lord, have we not prophesied in thy name? and in thy name have cast out devils? and in thy name done many wonderful works?

23 And then will I profess unto them, I never knew you: depart from me, ye that work iniquity.

12. "Those opposed to abortion cannot simply invoke God's will–they have to explain why abortion violates some principle that is accessible to people of all faiths."

Again so many Scriptures I could use, but I think this short one says it best.

Jeremiah 1:5King James Version (KJV)

5 Before I formed thee in the belly I knew thee; and before thou camest forth out of the womb I sanctified thee, and I ordained thee a prophet unto the nations.

13. On his support for civil unions for gay couples, and same sex marriage: "If people find that controversial then I would just refer them to the Sermon on the Mount."

1 Timothy 1:8-11King James Version (KJV)

8 But we know that the law is good, if a man use it lawfully;

9 Knowing this, that the law is not made for a righteous man, but for the lawless and disobedient, for the ungodly and for sinners, for unholy and profane, for murderers of fathers and murderers of mothers, for manslayers,

10 For whoremongers, for them that defile themselves with mankind, for menstealers, for liars, for perjured persons, and if there be any other thing that is contrary to sound doctrine;

11 According to the glorious gospel of the blessed God, which was committed to my trust.

14. "In our household, the Bible, the Koran and the Bhagavad Gita sat on the shelf alongside books of Greek and Norse and African mythology"

I have no idea how to address this. Too me it seems to suggest all of those books are good to find the path to Heaven. That is simply false.

15. "You got into these small towns in Pennsylvania and, like a lot of small towns in the Midwest, the jobs have been gone now for 25 years and nothing's replaced them. And they fell through the Clinton Administration, and the Bush Administration, and each successive administration has said that somehow these communities are gonna regenerate and they have not. And it's not surprising then they get bitter, they cling to guns or religion or antipathy to people who aren't like them or anti-immigrant

sentiment or anti-trade sentiment as a way to explain their frustrations."

Where to begin... I do cling to my Bible. I do cling to my Faith in Jesus Christ. I do cling to my 2nd Amendment Rights. You will not deprive me of any of those. I cling to the promises of God, not some politicians who would rather lie than tell the Truth. I cling to the Faith I have that when Americans start putting God first again, God will bless this country again and the economy will come back.

2 Chronicles 7:14King James Version (KJV)

14 If my people, which are called by my name, shall humble themselves, and pray, and seek my face, and turn from their wicked ways; then will I hear from heaven, and will forgive their sin, and will heal their land.

16. "On Easter or Christmas Day, my mother might drag me to church, just as she dragged me to the Buddhist temple, the Chinese New Year celebration, the Shinto shrine, and ancient Hawaiian burial sites."

I assume here President Obama means again there is only one way to get to Heaven. Again, according to the Scriptures it simply is not so.

1 John 4:1-3King James Version (KJV)

4 Beloved, believe not every spirit, but try the spirits whether they are of God: because many false prophets are gone out into the world.

2 Hereby know ye the Spirit of God: Every spirit that confesseth that Jesus Christ is come in the flesh is of God:

3 And every spirit that confesseth not that Jesus Christ is come in the flesh is not of God: and this is that spirit of antichrist, whereof ye have heard that it should come; and even now already is it in the world.

17. "We have Jews, Muslims, Hindus, atheists, agnostics, Buddhists, and their own path to grace is one that we have to revere and respect as much as our own"

Nothing is wrong with respecting these different people of other Faiths. Nothing at all. That doesn't mean however, we should revere their path to grace. It simply is not Biblical. Jesus said, "I am the way, the truth, and the life: no man cometh unto the Father, but by me." Period.

18. "All of us have a responsibility to work for the day when the mothers of Israelis and Palestinians can see their children grow up without fear; when the Holy Land of the three great faiths is the place of peace that God intended it to be; when Jerusalem is a secure and lasting home for Jews and Christians and Muslims, and a place for all of the children of Abraham to mingle peacefully together as in the story of Isra— (applause) — as in the story of Isra, when Moses, Jesus, and Mohammed, peace be upon them, joined in prayer. (Applause.)"

19. "I believe that there are many paths to the same place, and that is a belief that there is a higher power, a belief that we are connected as a people"

Again President Obama you are simply wrong. Again Jesus said, "I am the way, the truth, and the life: no man cometh unto the Father, but by me." Either you have never really studied The Holy Bible, or you are a wolf in sheeps clothing. Which is it sir? You are the President of The United States of America. When you talk people listen. When you misconstrue what The Holy Bible says for political gain you are nothing more than a false prophet. A deceiver leading people astray. The worst of the worst.

1 John 2:18-27King James Version (KJV)

18 Little children, it is the last time: and as ye have heard that antichrist shall come, even now are there many antichrists; whereby we know that it is the last time.

19 They went out from us, but they were not of us; for if they had been of us, they would no doubt have continued with us: but they went out, that they might be made manifest that they were not all of us.

20 But ye have an unction from the Holy One, and ye know all things.

21 I have not written unto you because ye know not the truth, but because ye know it, and that no lie is of the truth.

22 Who is a liar but he that denieth that Jesus is the Christ? He is antichrist, that denieth the Father and the Son.

23 Whosoever denieth the Son, the same hath not the Father: he that acknowledgeth the Son hath the Father also.

24 Let that therefore abide in you, which ye have heard from the beginning. If that which ye have heard from the beginning shall remain in you, ye also shall continue in the Son, and in the Father.

25 And this is the promise that he hath promised us, even eternal life.

26 These things have I written unto you concerning them that seduce you.

27 But the anointing which ye have received of him abideth in you, and ye need not that any man teach you: but as the same anointing teacheth you of all things, and is truth, and is no lie, and even as it hath taught you, ye shall abide in him.

You have used your position of authority to mislead people and totally lead them astray. Everyone hope when you were elected you would help unite this country, instead you have divided worse than I have ever seen. I am old enough I was around during the Civil Rights movement and the Vietnam War so that is saying a lot.

You have been caught in lie after lie to the citizens of the country you were elected to lead and still you lie. Remember this, "If you like your Dr. you can keep your

Dr." Or how about this, "If you like your health plan you can keep your health plan."

June 6, 2009: "If you like the plan you have, you can keep it. If you like the doctor you have, you can keep your doctor, too. The only change you'll see are falling costs as our reforms take hold."

June 11, 2009: "No matter how we reform health care, I intend to keep this promise: If you like your doctor, you'll be able to keep your doctor; if you like your health care plan, you'll be able to keep your health care plan."

June 15, 2009: "I know that there are millions of Americans who are content with their health care coverage — they like their plan and, most importantly, they value their relationship with their doctor. They trust you. And that means that no matter how we reform health care, we will keep this promise to the American people: If you like your doctor, you will be able to keep your doctor, period. If you like your health care plan, you'll be able to keep your health care plan, period. No one will take it away, no matter what."

June 23, 2009. "If you like your plan and you like your doctor, you won't have to do a thing. You keep your plan. You keep your doctor."

July 15, 2009. "If you like your doctor or health care provider, you can keep them. If you like your health care plan, you can keep that too."

July 16, 2009: "if you've got health insurance, you like your doctor, you like your plan — you can keep your doctor, you can keep your plan. Nobody is talking about taking that away from you."

July 18, 2009: "Michelle and I don't want anyone telling us who our family's doctor should be – and no one should decide that for you either. Under our proposals, if you like your doctor, you keep your doctor. If you like your current insurance, you keep that insurance. Period, end of story."

July 21, 2009: "If you like your current plan, you will be able to keep it. Let me repeat that: If you like your plan, you'll be able to keep it."

July 23, 2009: "Reform will keep the government out of your health care decisions, giving you the option to keep your coverage if you're happy with it."

July 29, 2009: "I have been as clear as I can be. Under the reform I've proposed, if you like your doctor, you keep your doctor. If you like your health care plan, you keep your health care plan. These folks need to stop scaring everybody. Nobody is talking about you forcing … to change your plans."

Aug. 8, 2009: "Under the reforms we seek, if you like your doctor, you can keep your doctor. If you like your health care plan, you can keep your health care plan."

Aug. 11, 2009: "Under the reform we're proposing, if you like your doctor, you can keep your doctor. If you like your health care plan, you can keep your health care plan."

Aug. 14, 2009: "If you like your health care plan, you can keep your health care plan. This is not some government takeover. If you like your doctor, you can keep seeing your doctor. This is important."

Aug. 15, 2009: "No matter what you've heard, if you like your doctor or health care plan, you can keep it."

Aug. 15, 2009: "I just want to be completely clear about this. I keep on saying this but somehow folks aren't listening — if you like your health care plan, you keep your health care plan. Nobody is going to force you to leave your health care plan. If you like your doctor, you keep seeing your doctor."

Aug. 20, 2009: "No matter what you've heard, if you like your doctor, you can keep your doctor under the reform proposals that we've put forward. If you like your private health insurance plan, you can keep it."

Aug. 22, 2009: "Under the reform we seek, if you like your doctor, you can keep your doctor. If you like your private health insurance plan, you can keep your plan. Period."

March 3, 2010: "If you like your plan, you can keep your plan. If you like your doctor, you can keep your doctor. Because I can tell you that as the father of two young girls, I wouldn't want any plan that interferes with the relationship between a family and their doctor."

March 6, 2010: "What won't change when this bill is signed is this: If you like the insurance plan you have now, you can keep it. If you like your doctor, you can keep your doctor. Because nothing should get in the way of the relationship between a family and their doctor."

March 10, 2010: "If you like your plan, you can keep your plan. If you like your doctor, you can keep your doctor. I'm the father of two young girls –- I don't want anybody interfering between my family and their doctor."

March 15, 2010: "If you like your plan, you can keep your plan. If you like your doctor, you can keep your doctor. I don't want to interfere with people's relationships between them and their doctors."

March 19, 2010: "If you like your doctor, you're going to be able to keep your doctor. If you like your plan, keep your plan. I don't believe we should give government or the insurance companies more control over health care in America. I think it's time to give you, the American people, more control over your health."

You lied. Then when you lied, you lied to try to cover it up. Then when you were caught in that lie you lied again, then just stopped discussing it.

You lied about your belief on same sex marriage. To get elected you said you believed in the Biblical definition of marriage. Then you told us your position had evolved. Then David Axelrod wrote his book and we find out all along you were lying. You believed in same sex marriage all along but wanted to be electable.

These were not lies of omission President Obama. You intentionally lied to get your way. God calls that an abomination.

You started out trying to divide us along racial lines from almost your first day in office. It started out with dropping the voter intimidation case of the New Black Panther Party members. It was videotaped! It was on every news channel. There was already a plea deal worked out. It was evident to anyone the only reason for those charges to be dropped had to be race related.

Then to the Cambridge Police acting stupidly. Before you even had a clue what happened you were in front of the camera blaming the Police Department. That cost the taxpayers a beer summit at the Whitehouse.

Then to Trayvon Martin. Again before you had a clue what happened you were on the television blaming the white man, who was actually Hispanic. Once again you were proven wrong. You sent your racist Department of Justice to Florida and they couldn't even come up with a civil rights violation against Zimmerman, but the damage was done. Once again you acting stupidly drove the wedge between the races a little farther.

Then there was Michael Brown. You know the invented hands up don't shoot guy? Brown never surrendered with his hands up, and Wilson was justified in shooting Brown. That, according to your own racist Department of Justice. Once again the damage was done.

If President Obama really believes in God, if he really studies the Holy Bible then he has to understand the danger he is putting America in. President Obama you have turned your back on Israel and forced our Nation to turn its back on Israel. The Bible, our Lord warn against this. Not only in the Old Testament as some suggest but in the New Testament as well!

Romans 11King James Version (KJV)

11 I say then, Hath God cast away his people? God forbid. For I also am an Israelite, of the seed of Abraham, of the tribe of Benjamin.

2 God hath not cast away his people which he foreknew. Wot ye not what the scripture saith of Elias? how he maketh intercession to God against Israel saying,

3 Lord, they have killed thy prophets, and digged down thine altars; and I am left alone, and they seek my life.

4 But what saith the answer of God unto him? I have reserved to myself seven thousand men, who have not bowed the knee to the image of Baal.

5 Even so then at this present time also there is a remnant according to the election of grace.

6 And if by grace, then is it no more of works: otherwise grace is no more grace. But if it be of works, then it is no more grace: otherwise work is no more work.

7 What then? Israel hath not obtained that which he seeketh for; but the election hath obtained it, and the rest were blinded.

8 (According as it is written, God hath given them the spirit of slumber, eyes that they should not see, and ears that they should not hear;) unto this day.

9 And David saith, Let their table be made a snare, and a trap, and a stumblingblock, and a recompence unto them:

10 Let their eyes be darkened, that they may not see, and bow down their back alway.

11 I say then, Have they stumbled that they should fall? God forbid: but rather through their fall salvation is come unto the Gentiles, for to provoke them to jealousy.

12 Now if the fall of them be the riches of the world, and the diminishing of them the riches of the Gentiles; how much more their fulness?

13 For I speak to you Gentiles, inasmuch as I am the apostle of the Gentiles, I magnify mine office:

14 If by any means I may provoke to emulation them which are my flesh, and might save some of them.

15 For if the casting away of them be the reconciling of the world, what shall the receiving of them be, but life from the dead?

16 For if the firstfruit be holy, the lump is also holy: and if the root be holy, so are the branches.

17 And if some of the branches be broken off, and thou, being a wild olive tree, wert grafted in among them, and with them partakest of the root and fatness of the olive tree;

18 Boast not against the branches. But if thou boast, thou bearest not the root, but the root thee.

19 Thou wilt say then, The branches were broken off, that I might be grafted in.

20 Well; because of unbelief they were broken off, and thou standest by faith. Be not highminded, but fear:

21 For if God spared not the natural branches, take heed lest he also spare not thee.

22 Behold therefore the goodness and severity of God: on them which fell, severity; but toward thee, goodness, if thou continue in his goodness: otherwise thou also shalt be cut off.

23 And they also, if they abide not still in unbelief, shall be grafted in: for God is able to graft them in again.

24 For if thou wert cut out of the olive tree which is wild by nature, and wert grafted contrary to nature into a good olive tree: how much more shall these, which be the natural branches, be grafted into their own olive tree?

25 For I would not, brethren, that ye should be ignorant of this mystery, lest ye should be wise in your own conceits; that blindness in part is happened to Israel, until the fulness of the Gentiles be come in.

26 And so all Israel shall be saved: as it is written, There shall come out of Sion the Deliverer, and shall turn away ungodliness from Jacob:

27 For this is my covenant unto them, when I shall take away their sins.

28 As concerning the gospel, they are enemies for your sakes: but as touching the election, they are beloved for the father's sakes.

29 For the gifts and calling of God are without repentance.

30 For as ye in times past have not believed God, yet have now obtained mercy through their unbelief:

31 Even so have these also now not believed, that through your mercy they also may obtain mercy.

32 For God hath concluded them all in unbelief, that he might have mercy upon all.

33 O the depth of the riches both of the wisdom and knowledge of God! how unsearchable are his judgments, and his ways past finding out!

34 For who hath known the mind of the Lord? or who hath been his counsellor?

35 Or who hath first given to him, and it shall be recompensed unto him again?

36 For of him, and through him, and to him, are all things: to whom be glory for ever. Amen.

The question becomes why? What does the President have against Israel? If he really is a Christian, he should never turn his back on Israel. Is he as some suggest a Muslim? I don't think so. If he is he is no better Muslim as far as following the Quran than he is a Christian following the Bible. Even though he lied and said he was the closest thing to a Jew America had ever had for a President, he certainly isn't Jewish.

This question has worried me since he first begin to show his true colors to Israel. Why? I think we may have recently seen why. He spent 20 years listening to Reverend Wright preach. Wright recently said at the anniversary of the million man march that Jesus was a Palestinian. Really? I guess the "good Reverend" hasn't studied his Bible either.

The genealogy in the Bible is very clear. Jesus was not a Palestinian. He was born to Jewish parents from Nazareth, therefore He was a Nazarene. This is why some Muslims, not only ISIS, mark the houses of Christians with an Arabic N.

The "good Reverend" also has said he had to be very careful around President Obama talking about Jesus. Wright said since President Obama had spent some of his early years with part of his family who are Muslim, he was very uncomfortable with the thought of Jesus as the Son of God. I don't know but perhaps the Presidents stance towards Israel comes from spending part of his childhood with Muslim family members. Perhaps it came from Reverend Wrights Church.

I do know according to Scripture we need to be prepared. God warns us in the end times every nation will turn against Israel. I never thought America would, but President Obama and his minions have certainly moved the country in that direction.

Just recently, as this book was being prepared to go to the printer was new evidence of his administration turning on Israel. During the recent attacks on innocent Israeli citizens, John Kerry said, "What's happening is that unless we get going, a two-state solution could conceivably be stolen from everybody," in rallying for a "solution" that has been tried for decades without any progress. Then the Secretary of State excused Palestinian terrorists for their actions against Israeli Jews. "And there's been a massive increase in settlements over the course of the last years. Now you have this violence because there's a frustration that is growing, and a frustration among Israelis who don't see any movement," Kerry added.

The State Department Spokesperson, John Kirby said the U.S. has "seen some reports of [Israeli] security activity that could indicate the potential excessive use of force," and added, "we're always concerned about credible reports of excessive use of force against civilians, and we routinely raise our concerns about that." I would have to ask Admiral Kirby what constitutes excessive use of force when a country is defending its innocent citizens.

At the same briefing, Kirby said that the "status quo" on the Temple Mount in Jerusalem "has not been observed" – a statement that would seem to be siding with the Palestinian version of what is happening at the site.

It is important to realize The Temple Mount is not just an important site for Muslims. Long, long before there was ever an Islam, the Temple Mount was a Holy Site for the Jewish people. Over 600 years before there was a Muhammad it was an important site for Christians. Because Muhammad *dreamed* he was whisked away from Mecca one night, taken to the Temple Mount where he was taken up to visit the **7** Heavens it becomes the 3rd Holiest site in Islam?

According to the Bible (Genesis 22:1–14), God told Abraham to bring his son Isaac to the land of Moriah (meaning "Chosen by Yah") and offer him as a sacrifice on a mountain there. As Abraham was about to complete the sacrifice, God stopped him and provided a ram as a substitutionary sacrifice. In this same location, nearly 1,000 years later, God led Solomon to build the First Temple (2 Chronicles 3:1). David had identified this location as the place for worshiping God because it was here the plague was stayed when he confessed his sin, and he purchased the place so he could build an altar (1 Chronicles 21:18–26). Solomon's Temple stood until the Babylonians destroyed it in 586 BC. Zerubbabel led the efforts to build the Second Temple, which was completed in 516 BC, then enlarged by Herod the Great in 12 BC. The Second Temple was destroyed by the Romans in AD 70, fulfilling Jesus' words in Mark 13:1–2.

As anyone can see BHO has turned on Israel many times. From his comments on the pre-1967 borders to approving or sending people from his campaign to Israel to try to influence Israel's elections. The list goes on and on.

Have you ever looked at a map of the Biblical Israel? Have you seen the map of the Biblical Israel with modern day Israel? Modern Israel is a tiny dot in comparison to Biblical Israel and President Obama wants to shrink it even more?

In comparison, he has sent money to Kenya for a voter identification program, but vigorously opposed voter identification laws in America.

He defended the Muslim Brotherhood in Egypt. Including sending them hundreds of millions of our tax payer dollars. He and his administration defended them so vigorously attorneys in Egypt have been working to have him, his ambassador to Egypt at the time, and Hillary Clinton charged with supporting a terrorist organization.

He, Hillary, and John Kerry have made one of the worst deals in world history with the Mullahs of Iran. Israel begged the U.S. not to do this. Members of his own party begged him not to do this. National Security experts begged him not to. Many Iranian dissidents begged him not to do this. He did it anyway. Already the world is seeing repercussions from this horrible deal.

He restored relations with Cuba against much advice from Cuban Americans. In my opinion he did this for the purpose of closing Gitmo. Immediately after the announcement the Castro's said in order to fully restore diplomatic relations Gitmo must be returned to Cuba. If Gitmo is not closed by the end of his term watch for him to try to return Gitmo to Cuba with an executive order. Then once again he bypasses Congress and gets his way. The Islamic terrorists at Gitmo will have to be brought to the U.S. or turned loose.

We are back to the same question, why? Why does he side with Islam over Christianity? Why does he almost always side with the Palestinians, Islamic Jihad, Hamas, and Hezbollah over Israel? Why is his State Department relaxing rules to allow Muslim refugees from Iraq and Syria but leaving Christian refugees for ISIS to brutally murder or force to convert to Islam?

Maybe we can gain some insight from his own words about Islam:

1.) "The future must not belong to those who slander the prophet of Islam"

He has shown he really means this. Look at his reaction after the Benghazi attack and murder of 4 Americans including our Ambassador to Libya. In spite of all the pre attack warnings. In spite of the intelligence on the ground in Benghazi he blamed the attack on a stupid YouTube video trailer. When Islamic terrorists attacked the Charlie Hebdo office in France for the Muhammad cartoons he refused to go march in solidarity with the other world leaders.

2.) "The sweetest sound I know is the Muslim call to prayer"
Really? I wonder how the Christians living among ISIS, Boko Haram, Al-Shabaab, and the others feel about that comment.

3.) "We will convey our deep appreciation for the Islamic faith, which has done so much over the centuries to shape the world — including in my own country."
When we get right down to it, in some ways I guess that could be true. If not for Islam, the U.S. Marines wouldn't have the nickname leathernecks. If not for Islam we wouldn't have The Freedom Tower in New York City we would still have The World Trade Center twin towers.

4.) "As a student of history, I also know civilization's debt to Islam."
Qur'an (9:5) "But when the forbidden months are past, then fight and slay the Pagans wherever ye find them, and seize them, beleaguer them, and lie in wait for them in every stratagem (of war); but if they

repent, and establish regular prayers and practice regular charity, then open the way for them..."
I wonder if that verse from the Quran could be the debt?

5.) "Islam has a proud tradition of tolerance."
I imagine Jews, Christians, Buddhist, Hindus, Atheists, Agnostics, and Homosexual's around the world would beg to differ. Could these words from Muhammad himself be the tradition of tolerance our President was talking about? Bukhari (52:177) - Allah's Apostle said, "The Hour will not be established until you fight with the Jews, and the stone behind which a Jew will be hiding will say. "O Muslim! There is a Jew hiding behind me, so kill him." Sorry Mr. President but that doesn't sound very tolerant to me.

6.) "Islam has always been part of America"
I guess there is a little truth to this. Let us look at what our 2nd President wrote about Islam. In reference to the Islamic slave trade of Americans and Europeans by the Barbary states, Jefferson asked Tripoli's envoy to London, Ambassador Sidi Haji Abdrahaman, by what right he extorted money and took slaves in this way. He answered:

"The ambassador answered us that [the right] was founded on the Laws of the Prophet, that it was written in their Koran, that all nations who should not have answered their authority were sinners, that it was their right and duty to make war upon them wherever they could be found, and to make slaves of all they could take as prisoners, and that every Mussulman who should be slain in battle was sure to go to Paradise."

7.) "We will encourage more Americans to study in Muslim communities"
Why would we want to do that? One of the things that radical Muslim terrorist have been successful at in the past 14 years is attacks on schools. During the last major attack the students were asked their religion. If they were Christians they were brutally murdered. Why would he even say it?

8.) "These rituals remind us of the principles that we hold in common, and Islam's role in advancing justice,   progress, tolerance, and the dignity of all human beings."
This is one of Muhammad's rituals, one of his lessons of tolerance: Bukhari (8:387) - Allah's Apostle said, "I have been ordered to fight the people till they say: 'None has the right to be worshipped but Allah'. And if they say so, pray like our prayers, face our Qibla and slaughter as we slaughter, then their blood and property will be sacred to us and we will not interfere with them except legally."

9.) "America and Islam are not exclusive and need not be in competition. Instead, they overlap, and share common principles of justice and progress, tolerance and the dignity of all human beings."

Quran (8:67) - "It is not for a Prophet that he should have prisoners of war until he had made a great slaughter in the land..."
I think that says enough to refute his statement.

The list of things he has said about Islam goes on, but they are all about the same. They paint Islam in a positive peaceful picture which is simply not true. At the same time, he seems to seldom pass up an opportunity to paint Christianity or America in a negative picture. The question? Why?

As I have said many times, and received a lot of criticism for I do not think President Obama is a Muslim any more than I think he is a Christian. Yes I know that is controversial, but I have quoted the Scriptures earlier in this chapter to prove my point.

We don't need to hate him though, we need to pray for him.

Chapter 9 - The Immigration Issue

John Adams - "The general principles, on which the Fathers achieved independence, were the only Principles in which that beautiful Assembly of young Gentlemen could Unite, and these Principles only could be intended by them in their address, or by me in my answer.

And what were these general Principles? I answer, the general Principles of Christianity, in which all these Sects were United: And the general Principles of English and American Liberty, in which all those young Men United, and which had United all Parties in America, in Majorities sufficient to assert and maintain her Independence.

"Now I will avow, that I then believe, and now believe, that those general Principles of Christianity, are as eternal and immutable, as the Existence and Attributes of God; and that those Principles of Liberty, are as unalterable as human Nature and our terrestrial, mundane System."

--Adams wrote this on June 28, 1813, excerpt from a letter to Thomas Jefferson.

This chapter is going to get me in trouble with my conservative friends, but I write what God puts on my heart. Not to win a popularity contest. An issue that divides us and must be resolved in order to move the country forward and heal some of the divisiveness.

Again I am going to take what I feel to be the Biblical solution. I will take a lot of criticism from Conservatives and Liberals alike.

I go to Church with 3 young men from the same family. I want to tell you about these men. They are salt of the earth. I love these young men and would be honored to have either or all of them in my family. They are what we typically refer to as "Dreamers." Their parents, also great people brought them to the U.S. as very small children. They now, finally have legal status, thank God.

Make no mistake, these young men have been a tremendous asset to the Church and to the community. They are very patriotic to the U.S.A. They put God, Family and the U.S.A. first. They make me proud to say they are as American as anyone born here. They make me proud to call them friends. I can't understand how anyone could think it would be "right" to deport any member of this family. They are the prime example of what America is supposed to be about.

Just as this prime example of what is right and good about bringing good people into this country, there is the flip side. What happened in San Francisco earlier this year is a prime example of what is wrong with our immigration system.

Kathryn Steinle her father and a family friend on the waterfront of the Embarcadero, when a shot rang out and Kathryn hit the ground. As she lay on the pier fighting for her life, she kept saying, 'Dad, help me, help me." Her Dad rendered CPR once she stopped breathing until the paramedics arrived on the scene. Two hours later she was pronounced dead at the hospital.

What started as an innocent family outing for this beautiful young lady ended in a family tragedy. It also brought to attention the national disgrace of sanctuary cities and not enforcing our nation's laws. Miss Steinle was murdered by Francisco Sanchez, who is approximately 45 and whose last known address was in Texas. He spoke with homicide inspectors and was later jailed on suspicion of murder. Sanchez was on probation at the time of the murder. He had been deported either 5 or 6 times in the past. He admitted he was in San Francisco because of its status as a Sanctuary City.

Before I get into the Scripture and what God has given me as a reasonable solution, let me say to my Conservative friends, get real. You know Americans are never going to round up 12,000,000 to 17,000,000 people and ship them out of the U.S. Never will happen.

To my liberal friends, get real. You know we are a Nation of laws. A sovereign Nation. We are not going to just leave our borders wide open and let anyone in who wants in. Nor are we going to just give blanket Amnesty and citizenship to those already here.

There are common sense Biblical solutions to this situation that we as a country should be able to come together on. First to my liberal readers who say/ think Jesus would want us to just open our borders, let everyone in and all of those who are already here to stay here. No, wrong answer. It is illegal to be in this country without the proper permission. Doing so is a violation of federal law. This is what God says about obeying the law.

Romans 13:1-7King James Version (KJV)

13 Let every soul be subject unto the higher powers. For there is no power but of God: the powers that be are ordained of God.

2 Whosoever therefore resisteth the power, resisteth the ordinance of God: and they that resist shall receive to themselves damnation.

3 For rulers are not a terror to good works, but to the evil. Wilt thou then not be afraid of the power? do that which is good, and thou shalt have praise of the same:

4 For he is the minister of God to thee for good. But if thou do that which is evil, be afraid; for he beareth not the sword in vain: for he is the minister of God, a revenger to execute wrath upon him that doeth evil.

5 Wherefore ye must needs be subject, not only for wrath, but also for conscience sake.

6 For for this cause pay ye tribute also: for they are God's ministers, attending continually upon this very thing.

7 Render therefore to all their dues: tribute to whom tribute is due; custom to whom custom; fear to whom fear; honour to whom honour.

Titus 3:1 - Put them in mind to be subject to principalities and powers, to obey magistrates, to be ready to every good work,

Acts 5:29 - Then Peter and the [other] apostles answered and said, We ought to obey God rather than men.

Luke 20:25 - And he said unto them, Render therefore unto Caesar the things which be Caesar's, and unto God the things which be God's.

1 John 2:4 - He that saith, I know him, and keepeth not his commandments, is a liar, and the truth is not in him.

1 John 3:4 - Whosoever committeth sin transgresseth also the law: for sin is the transgression of the law.

1 Peter 2:14 - Or unto governors, as unto them that are sent by him for the punishment of evildoers, and for the praise of them that do well.

Crossing the border illegally. Overstaying your visa limit. Lying on your application all violate U.S. law.

Now for my Conservative friends who say we should seal the borders and kick them all out.

Matthew 5:7

Blessed are the merciful: for they shall obtain mercy.

Matthew 23:23

Woe unto you, scribes and Pharisees, hypocrites! for ye pay tithe of mint and anise and cummin, and have omitted the weightier matters of the law, judgment, mercy, and faith: these ought ye to have done, and not to leave the other undone.

Luke 10:37

And he said, He that shewed mercy on him. Then said Jesus unto him, Go, and do thou likewise.

Romans 11:31

Even so have these also now not believed, that through your mercy they also may obtain mercy.

James 2:13

For he shall have judgment without mercy, that hath shewed no mercy; and mercy rejoiceth against judgment.

So I ask my Conservative friends, how can you ask God for mercy, if you can't show mercy to a family like the family I wrote about at the beginning of the chapter? How can you proclaim to stand for Judeo Christian values, and yell send them all home?

The answer is going to be somewhere near the middle. First and foremost our borders must be sealed. That should not be an issue for those on the right or those on the left. It should be a National Security issue. We live in a time where terrorism is a very real threat. Border control should be a concern for every single one of us. We have to enforce immigration laws. We are a Nation of laws, we can't have politicians who enforce the laws they want to enforce and leave the rest. It is not right. It is not Biblical.

Once the borders are sealed, we should identify those who are here illegally. Do good background checks. If they are good citizens. If they have jobs and families and no criminal record why wouldn't we reward them with a pathway to citizenship?

If they have criminal records, if they are gangbangers. If they don't learn English and try to assimilate. If they don't work and simply try to live off welfare, food stamps and other benefits, send them home.

Chapter 10 – What has happened to the Church?

Samuel Adams

Signer of the Declaration of Independence and Father of the American Revolution

"And as it is our duty to extend our wishes to the happiness of the great family of man, I conceive that we cannot better express ourselves than by humbly supplicating the Supreme Ruler of the world that the rod of tyrants may be broken to pieces, and the oppressed made free again; that wars may cease in all the earth, and that the confusions that are and have been among nations may be overruled by promoting and speedily bringing on that holy and happy period when the kingdom of our Lord and Saviour Jesus Christ may be everywhere established, and all people everywhere willingly bow to the sceptre of Him who is Prince of Peace."

--As Governor of Massachusetts, Proclamation of a Day of Fast, March 20, 1797.

Much to my wife's dismay I write this chapter. I told her I wouldn't name names or Churches I get nasty messages from. I really am not going to use any particular person I get nasty messages from, so I didn't lie, but I do think as a Christian I must name a few of the organizations who are so wickedly leading Christians astray.

1.) Religious Coalition for Reproductive Choice

The mission of the Religious Coalition for Reproductive Choice is to be the leading religious voice for reproductive justice in the country.

> This is an organization whose members preach that abortion is Biblical. They go to abortion centers and bless them. They preach that conservative Bible preaching Christians are wrong for opposing abortion. Woe be unto these Ministers on the day of Judgement. In an earlier chapter we discussed the Biblical reasons abortion is wrong. Now let us look at what the Bible says about these false teachers.
>
> **2 Timothy 4:3-4King James Version (KJV)**
>
> 3 For the time will come when they will not endure sound doctrine; but after their own lusts shall they heap to themselves teachers, having itching ears;
>
> 4 And they shall turn away their ears from the truth, and shall be turned unto fables.
>
> **1 Timothy 6:3-5King James Version (KJV)**

3 If any man teach otherwise, and consent not to wholesome words, even the words of our Lord Jesus Christ, and to the doctrine which is according to godliness;

4 He is proud, knowing nothing, but doting about questions and strifes of words, whereof cometh envy, strife, railings, evil surmisings,

5 Perverse disputings of men of corrupt minds, and destitute of the truth, supposing that gain is godliness: from such withdraw thyself.
2 Corinthians 11:13-15King James Version (KJV)

13 For such are false apostles, deceitful workers, transforming themselves into the apostles of Christ.

14 And no marvel; for Satan himself is transformed into an angel of light.

15 Therefore it is no great thing if his ministers also be transformed as the ministers of righteousness; whose end shall be according to their works.

2 Peter 2King James Version (KJV)

2 But there were false prophets also among the people, even as there shall be false teachers among you, who privily shall bring in damnable heresies,

even denying the Lord that bought them, and bring upon themselves swift destruction.

2 And many shall follow their pernicious ways; by reason of whom the way of truth shall be evil spoken of.

3 And through covetousness shall they with feigned words make merchandise of you: whose judgment now of a long time lingereth not, and their damnation slumbereth not.

4 For if God spared not the angels that sinned, but cast them down to hell, and delivered them into chains of darkness, to be reserved unto judgment;

5 And spared not the old world, but saved Noah the eighth person, a preacher of righteousness, bringing in the flood upon the world of the ungodly;

6 And turning the cities of Sodom and Gomorrha into ashes condemned them with an overthrow, making them an ensample unto those that after should live ungodly;

7 And delivered just Lot, vexed with the filthy conversation of the wicked:

8 (For that righteous man dwelling among them, in seeing and hearing, vexed his righteous soul from day to day with their unlawful deeds;)

9 The Lord knoweth how to deliver the godly out of temptations, and to reserve the unjust unto the day of judgment to be punished:

10 But chiefly them that walk after the flesh in the lust of uncleanness, and despise government. Presumptuous are they, selfwilled, they are not afraid to speak evil of dignities.

11 Whereas angels, which are greater in power and might, bring not railing accusation against them before the Lord.

12 But these, as natural brute beasts, made to be taken and destroyed, speak evil of the things that they understand not; and shall utterly perish in their own corruption;

13 And shall receive the reward of unrighteousness, as they that count it pleasure to riot in the day time. Spots they are and blemishes, sporting themselves with their own deceivings while they feast with you;

14 Having eyes full of adultery, and that cannot cease from sin; beguiling unstable souls: an heart they have exercised with covetous practices; cursed children:

15 Which have forsaken the right way, and are gone astray, following the way of Balaam the son of Bosor, who loved the wages of unrighteousness;

16 But was rebuked for his iniquity: the dumb ass speaking with man's voice forbad the madness of the prophet.

17 These are wells without water, clouds that are carried with a tempest; to whom the mist of darkness is reserved for ever.

18 For when they speak great swelling words of vanity, they allure through the lusts of the flesh, through much wantonness, those that were clean escaped from them who live in error.

19 While they promise them liberty, they themselves are the servants of corruption: for of whom a man is overcome, of the same is he brought in bondage.

20 For if after they have escaped the pollutions of the world through the knowledge of the Lord and Saviour Jesus Christ, they are again entangled therein, and overcome, the latter end is worse with them than the beginning.

21 For it had been better for them not to have known the way of righteousness, than, after they have known it, to turn from the holy commandment delivered unto them.

22 But it is happened unto them according to the true proverb, The dog is turned to his own vomit again; and the sow that was washed to her wallowing in the mire.

There is no need in going back through all of the Scriptures that say marriage is between a man and a woman, (Gen. 2:18-25; Lev. 18:22; Matt. 19:3-6; Rom. 1:24-28; I Cor. 6:9-11; 7:1-5; Eph. 5:22-6:4; I Tim. 1:8-11), we covered that pretty well earlier in the book. I do think however we need to realize these Ministers and Churches who are performing these same sex marriages, or ordaining gay and lesbian Ministers really need to get in their Bibles and do a lot of Praying!

For those Ministers and Churches who do, I remind you there is a Judgement Day. You will be judged by the One who designed marriage as between woman and man. The Bible tells us you won't just be judged for your sin, but also for leading the flock astray.

2.) New Ways Ministry

A gay-positive ministry of advocacy and justice for lesbian, gay, bisexual, and transgender (LGBT) Catholics, and reconciliation within the larger Christian and civil communities.

Ephesians 5:9-12King James Version (KJV)

9 (For the fruit of the Spirit is in all goodness and righteousness and truth;)

10 Proving what is acceptable unto the Lord.

11 And have no fellowship with the unfruitful works of darkness, but rather reprove them.

12 For it is a shame even to speak of those things which are done of them in secret.

1 John 4:1-6King James Version (KJV)

4 Beloved, believe not every spirit, but try the spirits whether they are of God: because many false prophets are gone out into the world.

2 Hereby know ye the Spirit of God: Every spirit that confesseth that Jesus Christ is come in the flesh is of God:

3 And every spirit that confesseth not that Jesus Christ is come in the flesh is not of God: and this is that spirit of antichrist, whereof ye have heard that it should come; and even now already is it in the world.

4 Ye are of God, little children, and have overcome them: because greater is he that is in you, than he that is in the world.

5 They are of the world: therefore speak they of the world, and the world heareth them.

6 We are of God: he that knoweth God heareth us; he that is not of God heareth not us. Hereby know we the spirit of truth, and the spirit of error.

1 John 2:26-27King James Version (KJV)

26 These things have I written unto you concerning them that seduce you.

27 But the anointing which ye have received of him abideth in you, and ye need not that any man teach you: but as the same anointing teacheth you of all things, and is truth, and is no lie, and even as it hath taught you, ye shall abide in him.

Jude 4King James Version (KJV)

4 For there are certain men crept in unawares, who were before of old ordained to this condemnation, ungodly men, turning the grace of our God into lasciviousness, and denying the only Lord God, and our Lord Jesus Christ.

Sojourners

"Sojourners ministries grew out of the Sojourners Community, located in Southern Columbia Heights, an inner-city neighborhood in Washington, D.C.

The community began at Trinity Evangelical Divinity School in Deerfield, Illinois, in the early 1970s when a handful of students began meeting to discuss the relationship between their faith and political issues, particularly the Vietnam War. In 1971, the group decided to create a publication that would express their convictions and test whether other people of faith had similar beliefs."

"In the fall of 1975, the fledgling community moved to Washington, D.C., where both the community and the magazine took the name Sojourners. The biblical metaphor "sojourners" identifies God's people as pilgrims—fully present in the world but committed to a different order. The community lived together in common households, had a common purse, formed a worshipping community, got involved in neighborhood issues, organized national events on behalf of peace and justice and continued to publish the magazine."

The highlighted areas above are straight off of their web page. Not my words, their words. Basically Sojourners was created from a socialist commune, a cult. The main change in the organization since its inception is they don't all live together anymore.

I was discussing their beliefs with a Minister. Some of the things he said really got to me. One of the things I couldn't believe he would admit to is they don't think the Bible is the true word of God. They believe it is and as near as I can remember this is a quote, "The bible is a very difficult book to understand and to use because it is not internally consistent, it does not claim to be perfect, and it is mistranslated. Anyone who thinks that the bible is anything more than "useful" needs to go reexamine their life, their beliefs, and have their head examined."

Really? Really? Needless to say I was in shock.

I do not believe the Bible is like an all you can eat buffet. You take a little of this and a little of that and in some cultural beliefs, and do as you wish. I believe those who teach that are the ones we are warned about in the Bible. I also believe they are who will rush us in to the time God and John warn about in the Book of Revelation.

One can tell from their web site and all the places they discuss "social justice" and "culture" they do nothing more than use a blending of the Holy Bible, the culture beliefs of the day and *their* idea of a utopian society. It is just **not** Biblical.

Chapter 11 – Civil Disobedience

John Hancock

1st Signer of the Declaration of Independence

"Resistance to tyranny becomes the Christian and social duty of each individual. ... Continue steadfast and, with a proper sense of your dependence on God, nobly defend those rights which heaven gave, and no man ought to take from us."

--History of the United States of America, Vol. II, p. 229

I and other Pastors have been criticized from more liberal Pastors recently for supporting civil disobedience. It is really kind of funny when you think about it. These are the same Pastors who support sanctuary cities. The same ones who supported Dr. Martin Luther King and the civil rights movement. The same ones who support amnesty for illegal aliens. All actions of civil disobedience.

Are we to assume civil disobedience is Biblical if it's only used for causes liberals arc behind? They like to use Romans 13 as their Biblical reason for no civil disobedience. There are plenty of Biblical examples of civil disobedience.

The first example I found of civil disobedience in the Bible was in Exodus Chapter 1. When the Pharaoh ordered the Hebrew midwives to kill the sons born to the Hebrew women, they did not. Verse 17 says, "But the midwives feared God, and did not as the king of Egypt commanded them, but saved the men children alive." Verse 21 goes on to say, "And it came to pass, because the midwives feared God, that he made them houses." As you can see God not only approved of their civil disobedience, he rewarded them with houses!

In Joshua 2 we read of Rahab. When the king of Jericho ordered her to turn over the spies Joshua had sent into Jericho, she told him the men had already left. Of course they had not. Rahab had hid them on the roof of the house.

Rahab was not punished by God for her act of civil disobedience against the king of Jericho. She was rewarded with the safety of herself and her family.

One of the great acts of civil disobedience as well as a great act of faith is told of in Daniel 3. King Nebuchadnezzar passed a law that anytime a citizen of his kingdom heard music they were to fall down and worship the image he had made. The penalty for refusing to do this was to be thrown into a raging furnace and burned alive. Shadrach, Meshach, and Abednego refused.

Nebuchadnezzar had the fire built so hot it burned the men up who threw the three in the furnace. Nebuchadnezzar saw 4 men walking around in the furnace! He verse 25 he said, " Lo I see four men loose, walking in the midst of the fire, and they have no hurt; and the form of the fourth is like the Son of God."

Shadrach, Meshach, and Abednego were called out of the furnace. There was not a hair on their body damaged. Their clothes were not singed, nor was there a smell of fire on them.

They chose an act of Faith. An act of civil disobedience. God didn't punish them. In fact He protected them. Instead of being burned in the fire, the king promoted them.

We only have to go 3 chapters to find the next example of civil disobedience. Again a tremendous example of Faith and civil disobedience. This one involving Daniel. Because of greed and jealousy king Darius had been persuaded to pass a law against praying to any God for 30 days. The penalty for praying was to be thrown into the lion's den.

Daniel did not stop praying. They men who were jealous of Daniel reported him to king Darius. The king did not want to, but had no choice due to the law he had signed. He had Daniel put into the lion's den. The den was sealed and the king went to his quarters. The king stayed up all night fasting.

The next morning the king went to the lion's den and called out to Daniel. Daniel answered God had sent an Angel who had sealed the lions mouth. The king had him pulled from the den. There was not a scratch on him. Daniel was completely unharmed. God didn't punish

Daniel for his act of civil disobedience, God rewarded him for his act of Faith. The king had the men who had crafted the law and convinced him to sign in thrown into the lion's den. Their wives and children were also thrown into the den.

There are many acts of civil disobedience recorded in the Bible. From Moses being placed in the basket all the way to Revelation 13. Not taking the mark of the beast will be another tremendous act of civil disobedience.

Look on Governor Huckabee's twitter feed. Look at all the tweets from liberal Ministers who chastise him for defending Kim Davis the Kentucky County Clerk who refused to issue the same sex marriage licenses because of her Faith.

This isn't to say there will not be penalties for acts of civil disobedience. There have been for many Christians. Look at the times Dr. King was arrested. Look at how the Disciples were punished. There may well be costs for standing for what is right and Biblical. If so, just remember the rewards will be great.

Chapter 12 – ACLU and SPLC

James Monroe

5th U.S. President

"When we view the blessings with which our country has been favored, those which we now enjoy, and the means which we possess of handing them down unimpaired to our latest posterity, our attention is irresistibly drawn to the source from whence they flow.

Let us then, unite in offering our most grateful acknowledgments for these blessings to the Divine Author of All Good."

--Monroe made this statement in his 2nd Annual Message to Congress, November 16, 1818.

The Southern Poverty Law Center maintains a list of hate groups. Some of the groups on their list actually deserve to be. Should you go to their website however, I think you would be shocked at some they have included on the list. I will be shocked if this book doesn't get me added to the list. If not it will only be due to the fact the book doesn't sell enough copies to get their attention! Seems as if all you need to do in order to get on their list of hate groups is disagree with them.

As I said, some of the groups deserve to be listed. The KKK groups, the skinheads, the New Black Panthers, etc…, but where are the radical Hispanic groups? Why so many Christian groups on the list?

One of the so called "hate groups" they list is The Family Research Council. How can anyone list them as a hate group? This is the mission statement from their web page:

Vision and Mission Statements

Vision Statement:

Family Research Council's vision is a culture in which human life is valued, families flourish and religious liberty thrives.

Mission of Organization:

Family Research Council's mission is to advance faith, family and freedom in public policy and the culture from a Christian worldview.

That doesn't sound the least bit hateful to me. Their work is not based on hate either, nor is it based on any kind of phobia. The Family Research Council's work is based on Biblical principles.

The SPLC also lists American Family Association as a hate group. This is a little about them from their web site.

The mission of the American Family Association is to inform, equip, and activate individuals to strengthen the moral foundations of American culture, and give aid to the church here and abroad in its task of fulfilling the Great Commission.

PHILOSOPHICAL STATEMENT

The American Family Association believes that God has communicated absolute truth to mankind, and that all people are subject to the authority of God's Word at all times. Therefore AFA believes that a culture based on biblical truth best serves the well-being of our nation and our families, in accordance with the vision of our founding documents; and that personal transformation through the Gospel of Jesus Christ is the greatest agent of biblical change in any culture.

ACTION STATEMENT

The American Family Association acts to:

1.restrain evil by exposing the works of darkness

2.promote virtue by upholding in culture that which is right, true and good according to Scripture

3.convince individuals of sin and challenge them to seek Christ's grace and forgiveness

4.motivate people to take a stand on cultural and moral issues at the local, state and national levels

5.encourage Christians to bear witness to the love of Jesus Christ as they live their lives before the world

To that end, AFA spurs activism directed to:

- Preservation of Marriage and the Family

- Decency and Morality

- Sanctity of Human Life

I can see nothing in their site, nor anything in their work that should warrant them being listed as a hate group.

They have listed California Coalition for Immigration Reform, a group that was started to stop US Taxpayer funded benefits from being awarded to illegal immigrants. I have to admit I know very little about this group. I could however find nothing bad about them. Unless you are for open borders.

They also list Federation for American Immigration Reform. This is from their web site.

The Federation for American Immigration Reform (FAIR) is a national, nonprofit, public-interest, membership organization of concerned citizens who share a common belief that our nation's immigration policies must be reformed to serve the national interest.

FAIR seeks to improve border security, to stop illegal immigration, and to promote immigration levels consistent with the national interest—more traditional rates of about 300,000 a year.

With more than 250,000 members and supporters nationwide, FAIR is a non-partisan group whose membership runs the gamut from liberal to conservative.

Our grassroots networks help concerned citizens use their voices to speak up for effective, sensible immigration policies that work for America's best interests.

FAIR's publications and research are used by academics and government officials in preparing new legislation. National and international media regularly turn to us to understand the latest immigration developments and to shed light on this complex subject. FAIR has been called to testify on immigration bills before Congress more than any organization in America.

That certainly doesn't sound like a hate group to me. It appears Congress doesn't think so either. It would seem like all you have to do to be added to the SPLC hate group list is to stand for Conservative principles or for Biblical principles. As I have said, there are groups on the list who have earned their place. Many who also have no business being on the list. Just as when they placed Governor Mike Huckabee on the list. Fortunately after the public outcry they removed the Governor from their list.

The American Civil Liberties Union. I don't think there has ever been a more destructive organization in our country. To be sure, when they first started there was a need. As often occurs something can be started for the right reasons, then be taken over by ideological zealots and become a very bad thing. Such is the case with the ACLU and the SPLC.

The ACLU has fought harder than even atheists groups against Christianity in any public venue. From high school athletic teams having a prayer before or after a competition or game to Nativity scenes at Christmas or Crosses. If allowed they would wipe out any symbols of Christianity.

They have hurt our National Security, just as the SPLC has. With their views and lawsuits on illegal immigration and terrorism. The ACLU has been an enemy of the United States of America when it comes to terrorism. Everything from our drone policy, the no fly list, enhanced interrogation, and Gitmo.

The ACLU has had more to do with the recidivism rate among prisoners in our prisons and correctional facilities than any other organization. They have made it almost impossible for the Criminal Justice system to properly function. There is no telling how much money they have cost this country in legal fees to defend against their lawsuits. They have become bullies.

Many towns, cities, counties, school districts etc… simply cannot afford to fight them in court. They will often be forced to cave in to the demands of the ACLU even when the law is on their side. Large legal defense bills would bankrupt many of these small towns and organizations.

If ever there was an evil organization, the ACLU is.

Chapter 13 – The United States Constitution

The Constitution is the guide which I never will abandon.

George Washington

Please take a few minutes and read your Constitution.

The Constitution of the United States: A Transcription

Note: The following text is a transcription of the Constitution as it was inscribed by Jacob Shallus on parchment (the document on display in the Rotunda at the National Archives Museum.) Items that are highlighted have since been amended or superseded. The authenticated text of the Constitution can be found on the website of the Government Printing Office.

We the People of the United States, in Order to form a more perfect Union, establish Justice, insure domestic Tranquility, provide for the common defence, promote the general Welfare, and secure the Blessings of Liberty to ourselves and our Posterity, do ordain and establish this Constitution for the United States of America.

Article. I.

Section. 1.

All legislative Powers herein granted shall be vested in a
Congress of the United States, which shall consist of a
Senate and House of Representatives.

Section. 2.

The House of Representatives shall be composed of
Members chosen every second Year by the People of the
several States, and the Electors in each State shall have the
Qualifications requisite for Electors of the most numerous
Branch of the State Legislature.

No Person shall be a Representative who shall not have
attained to the Age of twenty five Years, and been seven
Years a Citizen of the United States, and who shall not,
when elected, be an Inhabitant of that State in which he
shall be chosen.

Representatives and direct Taxes shall be apportioned among the several States which may be included within this Union, according to their respective Numbers, which shall be determined by adding to the whole Number of free Persons, including those bound to Service for a Term of Years, and excluding Indians not taxed, three fifths of all other Persons. The actual Enumeration shall be made within three Years after the first Meeting of the Congress of the United States, and within every subsequent Term of ten Years, in such Manner as they shall by Law direct. The Number of Representatives shall not exceed one for every thirty Thousand, but each State shall have at Least one Representative; and until such enumeration shall be made, the State of New Hampshire shall be entitled to chuse three, Massachusetts eight, Rhode-Island and Providence Plantations one, Connecticut five, New-York six, New Jersey four, Pennsylvania eight, Delaware one, Maryland six, Virginia ten, North Carolina five, South Carolina five, and Georgia three.

When vacancies happen in the Representation from any State, the Executive Authority thereof shall issue Writs of Election to fill such Vacancies.

The House of Representatives shall chuse their Speaker and other Officers; and shall have the sole Power of Impeachment.

Section. 3.

The Senate of the United States shall be composed of two Senators from each State, chosen by the Legislature thereof, for six Years; and each Senator shall have one Vote.

Immediately after they shall be assembled in Consequence of the first Election, they shall be divided as equally as may be into three Classes. The Seats of the Senators of the first Class shall be vacated at the Expiration of the second Year, of the second Class at the Expiration of the fourth Year, and of the third Class at the Expiration of the sixth Year, so that one third may be chosen every second Year; and if Vacancies happen by Resignation, or otherwise, during the Recess of the Legislature of any State, the Executive thereof may make temporary Appointments until the next Meeting of the Legislature, which shall then fill such Vacancies.

No Person shall be a Senator who shall not have attained to the Age of thirty Years, and been nine Years a Citizen of the United States, and who shall not, when elected, be an Inhabitant of that State for which he shall be chosen.

The Vice President of the United States shall be President of the Senate, but shall have no Vote, unless they be equally divided.

The Senate shall chuse their other Officers, and also a President pro tempore, in the Absence of the Vice President, or when he shall exercise the Office of President of the United States.

The Senate shall have the sole Power to try all Impeachments. When sitting for that Purpose, they shall be on Oath or Affirmation. When the President of the United States is tried, the Chief Justice shall preside: And no Person shall be convicted without the Concurrence of two thirds of the Members present.

Judgment in Cases of Impeachment shall not extend further than to removal from Office, and disqualification to hold and enjoy any Office of honor, Trust or Profit under the United States: but the Party convicted shall nevertheless be liable and subject to Indictment, Trial, Judgment and Punishment, according to Law.

Section. 4.

The Times, Places and Manner of holding Elections for Senators and Representatives, shall be prescribed in each State by the Legislature thereof; but the Congress may at any time by Law make or alter such Regulations, except as to the Places of chusing Senators.

The Congress shall assemble at least once in every Year, and such Meeting shall be on the first Monday in December, unless they shall by Law appoint a different Day.

Section. 5.

Each House shall be the Judge of the Elections, Returns and Qualifications of its own Members, and a Majority of each shall constitute a Quorum to do Business; but a smaller Number may adjourn from day to day, and may be authorized to compel the Attendance of absent Members, in such Manner, and under such Penalties as each House may provide.

Each House may determine the Rules of its Proceedings, punish its Members for disorderly Behaviour, and, with the Concurrence of two thirds, expel a Member.

Each House shall keep a Journal of its Proceedings, and from time to time publish the same, excepting such Parts as may in their Judgment require Secrecy; and the Yeas and Nays of the Members of either House on any question shall, at the Desire of one fifth of those Present, be entered on the Journal.

Neither House, during the Session of Congress, shall, without the Consent of the other, adjourn for more than three days, nor to any other Place than that in which the two Houses shall be sitting.

Section. 6.

The Senators and Representatives shall receive a Compensation for their Services, to be ascertained by Law, and paid out of the Treasury of the United States. They shall in all Cases, except Treason, Felony and Breach of the Peace, be privileged from Arrest during their Attendance at the Session of their respective Houses, and in going to and returning from the same; and for any Speech or Debate in either House, they shall not be questioned in any other Place.

No Senator or Representative shall, during the Time for which he was elected, be appointed to any civil Office under the Authority of the United States, which shall have been created, or the Emoluments whereof shall have been encreased during such time; and no Person holding any Office under the United States, shall be a Member of either House during his Continuance in Office.

Section. 7.

All Bills for raising Revenue shall originate in the House of Representatives; but the Senate may propose or concur with Amendments as on other Bills.

Every Bill which shall have passed the House of Representatives and the Senate, shall, before it become a Law, be presented to the President of the United States; If he approve he shall sign it, but if not he shall return it, with his Objections to that House in which it shall have originated, who shall enter the Objections at large on their Journal, and proceed to reconsider it. If after such Reconsideration two thirds of that House shall agree to pass the Bill, it shall be sent, together with the Objections, to the other House, by which it shall likewise be reconsidered, and if approved by two thirds of that House, it shall become a Law. But in all such Cases the Votes of both Houses shall be determined by yeas and Nays, and the Names of the Persons voting for and against the Bill shall be entered on the Journal of each House respectively. If any Bill shall not be returned by the President within ten Days (Sundays excepted) after it shall have been presented to him, the Same shall be a Law, in like Manner as if he had signed it, unless the Congress by their Adjournment prevent its Return, in which Case it shall not be a Law.

Every Order, Resolution, or Vote to which the Concurrence of the Senate and House of Representatives may be necessary (except on a question of Adjournment) shall be presented to the President of the United States; and before the Same shall take Effect, shall be approved by him, or being disapproved by him, shall be repassed by two thirds of the Senate and House of Representatives, according to the Rules and Limitations prescribed in the Case of a Bill.

Section. 8.

The Congress shall have Power To lay and collect Taxes, Duties, Imposts and Excises, to pay the Debts and provide for the common Defence and general Welfare of the United States; but all Duties, Imposts and Excises shall be uniform throughout the United States;

To borrow Money on the credit of the United States;

To regulate Commerce with foreign Nations, and among the several States, and with the Indian Tribes;

To establish an uniform Rule of Naturalization, and uniform Laws on the subject of Bankruptcies throughout the United States;

To coin Money, regulate the Value thereof, and of foreign Coin, and fix the Standard of Weights and Measures;

To provide for the Punishment of counterfeiting the Securities and current Coin of the United States;

To establish Post Offices and post Roads;

To promote the Progress of Science and useful Arts, by securing for limited Times to Authors and Inventors the exclusive Right to their respective Writings and Discoveries;

To constitute Tribunals inferior to the supreme Court;

To define and punish Piracies and Felonies committed on the high Seas, and Offences against the Law of Nations;

To declare War, grant Letters of Marque and Reprisal, and make Rules concerning Captures on Land and Water;

To raise and support Armies, but no Appropriation of Money to that Use shall be for a longer Term than two Years;

To provide and maintain a Navy;

To make Rules for the Government and Regulation of the land and naval Forces;

To provide for calling forth the Militia to execute the Laws of the Union, suppress Insurrections and repel Invasions;

To provide for organizing, arming, and disciplining, the Militia, and for governing such Part of them as may be employed in the Service of the United States, reserving to the States respectively, the Appointment of the Officers, and the Authority of training the Militia according to the discipline prescribed by Congress;

To exercise exclusive Legislation in all Cases whatsoever, over such District (not exceeding ten Miles square) as may, by Cession of particular States, and the Acceptance of Congress, become the Seat of the Government of the United States, and to exercise like Authority over all Places purchased by the Consent of the Legislature of the State in which the Same shall be, for the Erection of Forts, Magazines, Arsenals, dock-Yards, and other needful Buildings;—And

To make all Laws which shall be necessary and proper for carrying into Execution the foregoing Powers, and all other Powers vested by this Constitution in the Government of the United States, or in any Department or Officer thereof.

Section. 9.

The Migration or Importation of such Persons as any of the States now existing shall think proper to admit, shall not be prohibited by the Congress prior to the Year one thousand eight hundred and eight, but a Tax or duty may be imposed on such Importation, not exceeding ten dollars for each Person.

The Privilege of the Writ of Habeas Corpus shall not be suspended, unless when in Cases of Rebellion or Invasion the public Safety may require it.

No Bill of Attainder or ex post facto Law shall be passed.

No Capitation, or other direct, Tax shall be laid, unless in Proportion to the Census or enumeration herein before directed to be taken.

No Tax or Duty shall be laid on Articles exported from any State.

No Preference shall be given by any Regulation of Commerce or Revenue to the Ports of one State over those of another: nor shall Vessels bound to, or from, one State, be obliged to enter, clear, or pay Duties in another.

No Money shall be drawn from the Treasury, but in Consequence of Appropriations made by Law; and a regular Statement and Account of the Receipts and Expenditures of all public Money shall be published from time to time.

No Title of Nobility shall be granted by the United States: And no Person holding any Office of Profit or Trust under them, shall, without the Consent of the Congress, accept of any present, Emolument, Office, or Title, of any kind whatever, from any King, Prince, or foreign State.

Section. 10.

No State shall enter into any Treaty, Alliance, or Confederation; grant Letters of Marque and Reprisal; coin Money; emit Bills of Credit; make any Thing but gold and silver Coin a Tender in Payment of Debts; pass any Bill of Attainder, ex post facto Law, or Law impairing the Obligation of Contracts, or grant any Title of Nobility.

No State shall, without the Consent of the Congress, lay any Imposts or Duties on Imports or Exports, except what may be absolutely necessary for executing it's inspection Laws: and the net Produce of all Duties and Imposts, laid by any State on Imports or Exports, shall be for the Use of the Treasury of the United States; and all such Laws shall be subject to the Revision and Controul of the Congress.

No State shall, without the Consent of Congress, lay any Duty of Tonnage, keep Troops, or Ships of War in time of Peace, enter into any Agreement or Compact with another State, or with a foreign Power, or engage in War, unless actually invaded, or in such imminent Danger as will not admit of delay.

Article. II.

Section. 1.

The executive Power shall be vested in a President of the United States of America. He shall hold his Office during the Term of four Years, and, together with the Vice President, chosen for the same Term, be elected, as follows

Each State shall appoint, in such Manner as the Legislature thereof may direct, a Number of Electors, equal to the whole Number of Senators and Representatives to which the State may be entitled in the Congress: but no Senator or Representative, or Person holding an Office of Trust or Profit under the United States, shall be appointed an Elector.

The Electors shall meet in their respective States, and vote by Ballot for two Persons, of whom one at least shall not be an Inhabitant of the same State with themselves. And they shall make a List of all the Persons voted for, and of the Number of Votes for each; which List they shall sign and certify, and transmit sealed to the Seat of the Government of the United States, directed to the President of the Senate. The President of the Senate shall, in the Presence of the Senate and House of Representatives, open all the Certificates, and the Votes shall then be counted. The Person having the greatest Number of Votes shall be the President, if such Number be a Majority of the whole Number of Electors appointed; and if there be more than one who have such Majority, and have an equal Number of Votes, then the House of Representatives shall immediately chuse by Ballot one of them for President; and if no Person have a Majority, then from the five highest on the List the said House shall in like Manner chuse the President. But in chusing the President, the Votes shall be taken by States, the Representation from each State having one Vote; A quorum for this Purpose shall consist of a Member or Members from two thirds of the States, and a Majority of all the States shall be necessary to a Choice. In every Case, after the Choice of the President, the Person having the greatest Number of Votes of the Electors shall be the Vice President. But if there should remain two or more who have equal Votes, the Senate shall chuse from them by Ballot the Vice President.

The Congress may determine the Time of chusing the Electors, and the Day on which they shall give their Votes; which Day shall be the same throughout the United States.

No Person except a natural born Citizen, or a Citizen of the United States, at the time of the Adoption of this Constitution, shall be eligible to the Office of President; neither shall any Person be eligible to that Office who shall not have attained to the Age of thirty five Years, and been fourteen Years a Resident within the United States.

In Case of the Removal of the President from Office, or of his Death, Resignation, or Inability to discharge the Powers and Duties of the said Office, the Same shall devolve on the Vice President, and the Congress may by Law provide for the Case of Removal, Death, Resignation or Inability, both of the President and Vice President, declaring what Officer shall then act as President, and such Officer shall act accordingly, until the Disability be removed, or a President shall be elected.

The President shall, at stated Times, receive for his Services, a Compensation, which shall neither be encreased nor diminished during the Period for which he shall have been elected, and he shall not receive within that Period any other Emolument from the United States, or any of them.

Before he enter on the Execution of his Office, he shall take the following Oath or Affirmation:—"I do solemnly swear (or affirm) that I will faithfully execute the Office of President of the United States, and will to the best of my Ability, preserve, protect and defend the Constitution of the United States."

Section. 2.

The President shall be Commander in Chief of the Army and Navy of the United States, and of the Militia of the several States, when called into the actual Service of the United States; he may require the Opinion, in writing, of the principal Officer in each of the executive Departments, upon any Subject relating to the Duties of their respective Offices, and he shall have Power to grant Reprieves and Pardons for Offences against the United States, except in Cases of Impeachment.

He shall have Power, by and with the Advice and Consent of the Senate, to make Treaties, provided two thirds of the Senators present concur; and he shall nominate, and by and with the Advice and Consent of the Senate, shall appoint Ambassadors, other public Ministers and Consuls, Judges of the supreme Court, and all other Officers of the United States, whose Appointments are not herein otherwise provided for, and which shall be established by Law: but the Congress may by Law vest the Appointment of such inferior Officers, as they think proper, in the President alone, in the Courts of Law, or in the Heads of Departments.

The President shall have Power to fill up all Vacancies that may happen during the Recess of the Senate, by granting Commissions which shall expire at the End of their next Session.

Section. 3.

He shall from time to time give to the Congress Information of the State of the Union, and recommend to their Consideration such Measures as he shall judge necessary and expedient; he may, on extraordinary Occasions, convene both Houses, or either of them, and in Case of Disagreement between them, with Respect to the Time of Adjournment, he may adjourn them to such Time as he shall think proper; he shall receive Ambassadors and other public Ministers; he shall take Care that the Laws be faithfully executed, and shall Commission all the Officers of the United States.

Section. 4.

The President, Vice President and all civil Officers of the United States, shall be removed from Office on Impeachment for, and Conviction of, Treason, Bribery, or other high Crimes and Misdemeanors.

Article III.

Section. 1.

The judicial Power of the United States, shall be vested in one supreme Court, and in such inferior Courts as the Congress may from time to time ordain and establish. The Judges, both of the supreme and inferior Courts, shall hold their Offices during good Behaviour, and shall, at stated Times, receive for their Services, a Compensation, which shall not be diminished during their Continuance in Office.

Section. 2.

The judicial Power shall extend to all Cases, in Law and Equity, arising under this Constitution, the Laws of the United States, and Treaties made, or which shall be made, under their Authority;—to all Cases affecting Ambassadors, other public Ministers and Consuls;—to all Cases of admiralty and maritime Jurisdiction;—to Controversies to which the United States shall be a Party;—to Controversies between two or more States;—between a State and Citizens of another State,—between Citizens of different States,—between Citizens of the same State claiming Lands under Grants of different States, and between a State, or the Citizens thereof, and foreign States, Citizens or Subjects.

In all Cases affecting Ambassadors, other public Ministers and Consuls, and those in which a State shall be Party, the supreme Court shall have original Jurisdiction. In all the other Cases before mentioned, the supreme Court shall have appellate Jurisdiction, both as to Law and Fact, with such Exceptions, and under such Regulations as the Congress shall make.

The Trial of all Crimes, except in Cases of Impeachment, shall be by Jury; and such Trial shall be held in the State where the said Crimes shall have been committed; but when not committed within any State, the Trial shall be at such Place or Places as the Congress may by Law have directed.

Section. 3.

Treason against the United States, shall consist only in levying War against them, or in adhering to their Enemies, giving them Aid and Comfort. No Person shall be convicted of Treason unless on the Testimony of two Witnesses to the same overt Act, or on Confession in open Court.

The Congress shall have Power to declare the Punishment of Treason, but no Attainder of Treason shall work Corruption of Blood, or Forfeiture except during the Life of the Person attainted.

Article. IV.

Section. 1.

Full Faith and Credit shall be given in each State to the public Acts, Records, and judicial Proceedings of every other State. And the Congress may by general Laws prescribe the Manner in which such Acts, Records and Proceedings shall be proved, and the Effect thereof.

Section. 2.

The Citizens of each State shall be entitled to all Privileges and Immunities of Citizens in the several States.

A Person charged in any State with Treason, Felony, or other Crime, who shall flee from Justice, and be found in another State, shall on Demand of the executive Authority of the State from which he fled, be delivered up, to be removed to the State having Jurisdiction of the Crime.

No Person held to Service or Labour in one State, under the Laws thereof, escaping into another, shall, in Consequence of any Law or Regulation therein, be discharged from such Service or Labour, but shall be delivered up on Claim of the Party to whom such Service or Labour may be due.

Section. 3.

New States may be admitted by the Congress into this Union; but no new State shall be formed or erected within the Jurisdiction of any other State; nor any State be formed by the Junction of two or more States, or Parts of States, without the Consent of the Legislatures of the States concerned as well as of the Congress.

The Congress shall have Power to dispose of and make all needful Rules and Regulations respecting the Territory or other Property belonging to the United States; and nothing in this Constitution shall be so construed as to Prejudice any Claims of the United States, or of any particular State.

Section. 4.

The United States shall guarantee to every State in this Union a Republican Form of Government, and shall protect each of them against Invasion; and on Application of the Legislature, or of the Executive (when the

Legislature cannot be convened), against domestic Violence.

Article. V.

The Congress, whenever two thirds of both Houses shall deem it necessary, shall propose Amendments to this Constitution, or, on the Application of the Legislatures of two thirds of the several States, shall call a Convention for proposing Amendments, which, in either Case, shall be valid to all Intents and Purposes, as Part of this Constitution, when ratified by the Legislatures of three fourths of the several States, or by Conventions in three fourths thereof, as the one or the other Mode of Ratification may be proposed by the Congress; Provided that no Amendment which may be made prior to the Year One thousand eight hundred and eight shall in any Manner affect the first and fourth Clauses in the Ninth Section of the first Article; and that no State, without its Consent, shall be deprived of its equal Suffrage in the Senate.

Article. VI.

All Debts contracted and Engagements entered into, before the Adoption of this Constitution, shall be as valid against the United States under this Constitution, as under the Confederation.

This Constitution, and the Laws of the United States which shall be made in Pursuance thereof; and all Treaties made, or which shall be made, under the Authority of the United States, shall be the supreme Law of the Land; and the Judges in every State shall be bound thereby, any Thing in the Constitution or Laws of any State to the Contrary notwithstanding.

The Senators and Representatives before mentioned, and the Members of the several State Legislatures, and all executive and judicial Officers, both of the United States and of the several States, shall be bound by Oath or Affirmation, to support this Constitution; but no religious Test shall ever be required as a Qualification to any Office or public Trust under the United States.

Article. VII.

The Ratification of the Conventions of nine States, shall be sufficient for the Establishment of this Constitution between the States so ratifying the Same.

The Word, "the," being interlined between the seventh and eighth Lines of the first Page, The Word "Thirty" being partly written on an Erazure in the fifteenth Line of the first Page, The Words "is tried" being interlined between the thirty second and thirty third Lines of the first Page and the Word "the" being interlined between the forty third and forty fourth Lines of the second Page.

Attest William Jackson Secretary

done in Convention by the Unanimous Consent of the States present the Seventeenth Day of September in the Year of our Lord one thousand seven hundred and Eighty seven and of the Independance of the United States of America the Twelfth In witness whereof We have hereunto subscribed our Names,

G°. Washington

 Presidt and deputy from Virginia

Delaware

Geo: Read

Gunning Bedford jun

John Dickinson

Richard Bassett

Jaco: Broom

Maryland

James McHenry

Dan of St Thos. Jenifer

Danl. Carroll

Virginia

John Blair

James Madison Jr.

North Carolina

Wm. Blount

Richd. Dobbs Spaight

Hu Williamson

South Carolina

J. Rutledge

Charles Cotesworth Pinckney

Charles Pinckney

Pierce Butler

Georgia

William Few

Abr Baldwin

New Hampshire

John Langdon

Nicholas Gilman

Massachusetts

Nathaniel Gorham

Rufus King

Connecticut

Wm. Saml. Johnson

Roger Sherman

New York

Alexander Hamilton

New Jersey

Wil: Livingston

David Brearley

Wm. Paterson

Jona: Dayton

Pensylvania

B Franklin

Thomas Mifflin

Robt. Morris

Geo. Clymer

Thos. FitzSimons

Jared Ingersoll

James Wilson

Gouv Morris

The Bill of Rights – Full Text

Amendment I

Congress shall make no law respecting an establishment of religion, or prohibiting the free exercise thereof; or abridging the freedom of speech, or of the press; or the right of the people peaceably to assemble, and to petition the government for a redress of grievances.

Amendment II

A well regulated militia, being necessary to the security of a free state, the right of the people to keep and bear arms, shall not be infringed.

Amendment III

No soldier shall, in time of peace be quartered in any house, without the consent of the owner, nor in time of war, but in a manner to be prescribed by law.

Amendment IV

The right of the people to be secure in their persons, houses, papers, and effects, against unreasonable searches and seizures, shall not be violated, and no warrants shall issue, but upon probable cause, supported by oath or affirmation, and particularly describing the place to be searched, and the persons or things to be seized.

Amendment V

No person shall be held to answer for a capital, or otherwise infamous crime, unless on a presentment or indictment of a grand jury, except in cases arising in the land or naval forces, or in the militia, when in actual service in time of war or public danger; nor shall any person be subject for the same offense to be twice put in jeopardy of life or limb; nor shall be compelled in any criminal case to be a witness against himself, nor be deprived of life, liberty, or property, without due process of law; nor shall private property be taken for public use, without just compensation.

Amendment VI

In all criminal prosecutions, the accused shall enjoy the right to a speedy and public trial, by an impartial jury of the state and district wherein the crime shall have been committed, which district shall have been previously ascertained by law, and to be informed of the nature and cause of the accusation; to be confronted with the witnesses against him; to have compulsory process for obtaining witnesses in his favor, and to have the assistance of counsel for his defense.

Amendment VII

In suits at common law, where the value in controversy shall exceed twenty dollars, the right of trial by jury shall be preserved, and no fact tried by a jury, shall be otherwise reexamined in any court of the United States, than according to the rules of the common law.

Amendment VIII

Excessive bail shall not be required, nor excessive fines imposed, nor cruel and unusual punishments inflicted.

Amendment IX

The enumeration in the Constitution, of certain rights, shall not be construed to deny or disparage others retained by the people.

Amendment X

The powers not delegated to the United States by the Constitution, nor prohibited by it to the states, are reserved to the states respectively, or to the people.

In my opinion, The United States Constitution and Bill of Rights are, next to The Holy Bible, the most important document ever written. I hope you took the time to read it. Without God and this document America would not be what it has been.

We citizens, over the past 50 – 60 years have allowed Judges, Lawyers and politicians to interpret, ignore it, and try to change it. It is time we say enough. Words mean things. It is not right for Judges, Lawyers, or Politicians to go back over 200 years and say well the Founding Fathers meant this or that. They meant what they wrote. Period.

There is nothing, absolutely nothing in that document to prevent prayer in schools. To prevent a governing body from opening a meeting in prayer. There is nothing in that document to prevent a Nativity Scene on the courthouse lawn at Christmas. There is nothing to prevent the 10 Commandments from being displayed in a government building. There is nothing in it to prevent a cross from being displayed.

We have allowed the ACLU, Lawyers, Judges and politicians to do that under the false narrative of that is what the Constitution says. No it isn't. Show me where?

It says, "Congress shall make no law respecting an establishment of religion, or prohibiting the free exercise thereof". Period. Attorneys and Judges with an agenda have used those 16 words that should guarantee our rights to strip us of our rights. What it says is very clear. It needs no interpretation. Praying in schools is not establishing a religion. Prohibiting that prayer is prohibiting the free exercise thereof.

The Second Amendment says, "A well regulated militia, being necessary to the security of a free state, the right of the people to keep and bear arms, shall not be infringed." It plainly states, the right of the people to keep and bear arms, **shall not be infringed.** Period. It doesn't say it must be in a militia. It doesn't say for hunting. It doesn't say it can only have the capacity for so many bullets, nor that it has to be registered. It doesn't say you must have a permit, go through a background check or anything else. It says shall not be infringed.

Take a look at what the Founders thought of the Second Amendment.

"A free people ought not only to be armed, but disciplined..."

 - George Washington, First Annual Address, to both House of Congress, January 8, 1790

"No free man shall ever be debarred the use of arms."

 - Thomas Jefferson, Virginia Constitution, Draft 1, 1776

"I prefer dangerous freedom over peaceful slavery."

- Thomas Jefferson, letter to James Madison, January 30, 1787

"What country can preserve its liberties if their rulers are not warned from time to time that their people preserve the spirit of resistance. Let them take arms."

- Thomas Jefferson, letter to James Madison, December 20, 1787

"The laws that forbid the carrying of arms are laws of such a nature. They disarm only those who are neither inclined nor determined to commit crimes.... Such laws make things worse for the assaulted and better for the assailants; they serve rather to encourage than to prevent homicides, for an unarmed man may be attacked with greater confidence than an armed man."

- Thomas Jefferson, Commonplace Book (quoting 18th century criminologist Cesare Beccaria), 1774-1776

"A strong body makes the mind strong. As to the species of exercises, I advise the gun. While this gives moderate exercise to the body, it gives boldness, enterprise and independence to the mind. Games played with the ball, and others of that nature, are too violent for the body and stamp no character on the mind. Let your gun therefore be your constant companion of your walks." - Thomas Jefferson, letter to Peter Carr, August 19, 1785

"The Constitution of most of our states (and of the United States) assert that all power is inherent in the people; that they may exercise it by themselves; that it is their right and duty to be at all times armed."

- Thomas Jefferson, letter to to John Cartwright, 5 June 1824

"On every occasion [of Constitutional interpretation] let us carry ourselves back to the time when the Constitution was adopted, recollect the spirit manifested in the debates, and instead of trying [to force] what meaning may be squeezed out of the text, or invented against it, [instead let us] conform to the probable one in which it was passed."

- Thomas Jefferson, letter to William Johnson, 12 June 1823

"I enclose you a list of the killed, wounded, and captives of the enemy from the commencement of hostilities at Lexington in April, 1775, until November, 1777, since which there has been no event of any consequence ... I think that upon the whole it has been about one half the number lost by them, in some instances more, but in others less. This difference is ascribed to our superiority in taking aim when we fire; every soldier in our army having been intimate with his gun from his infancy."

 - Thomas Jefferson, letter to Giovanni Fabbroni, June 8, 1778

"They that can give up essential liberty to obtain a little temporary safety deserve neither liberty nor safety."

 - Benjamin Franklin, Historical Review of Pennsylvania, 1759

"To disarm the people...[i]s the most effectual way to enslave them."

- George Mason, referencing advice given to the British Parliament by Pennsylvania governor Sir William Keith, The Debates in the Several State Conventions on the Adooption of the Federal Constitution, June 14, 1788

"I ask who are the militia? They consist now of the whole people, except a few public officers."

- George Mason, Address to the Virginia Ratifying Convention, June 4, 1788

"Before a standing army can rule, the people must be disarmed, as they are in almost every country in Europe. The supreme power in America cannot enforce unjust laws by the sword; because the whole body of the people are armed, and constitute a force superior to any band of regular troops."

- Noah Webster, An Examination of the Leading Principles of the Federal Constitution, October 10, 1787

"Besides the advantage of being armed, which the Americans possess over the people of almost every other nation, the existence of subordinate governments, to which the people are attached, and by which the militia officers are appointed, forms a barrier against the enterprises of ambition, more insurmountable than any which a simple government of any form can admit of."

- James Madison, Federalist No. 46, January 29, 1788

"The right of the people to keep and bear arms shall not be infringed. A well regulated militia, composed of the body of the people, trained to arms, is the best and most natural defense of a free country."

- James Madison, I Annals of Congress 434, June 8, 1789

"...the ultimate authority, wherever the derivative may be found, resides in the people alone..."

- James Madison, Federalist No. 46, January 29, 1788

"Necessity is the plea for every infringement of human freedom. It is the argument of tyrants; it is the creed of slaves."

- William Pitt (the Younger), Speech in the House of Commons, November 18, 1783

"A militia when properly formed are in fact the people themselves…and include, according to the past and general usuage of the states, all men capable of bearing arms… "To preserve liberty, it is essential that the whole body of the people always possess arms, and be taught alike, especially when young, how to use them."

- Richard Henry Lee, Federal Farmer No. 18, January 25, 1788

"Guard with jealous attention the public liberty. Suspect everyone who approaches that jewel. Unfortunately, nothing will preserve it but downright force. Whenever you give up that force, you are ruined.... The great object is that every man be armed. Everyone who is able might have a gun."

- Patrick Henry, Speech to the Virginia Ratifying Convention, June 5, 1778

"This may be considered as the true palladium of liberty.... The right of self defense is the first law of nature: in most governments it has been the study of rulers to confine this right within the narrowest limits possible. Wherever standing armies are kept up, and the right of the people to keep and bear arms is, under any color or pretext whatsoever, prohibited, liberty, if not already annihilated, is on the brink of destruction."

- St. George Tucker, Blackstone's Commentaries on the Laws of England, 1803

"The supposed quietude of a good man allures the ruffian; while on the other hand, arms, like law, discourage and keep the invader and the plunderer in awe, and preserve order in the world as well as property. The balance ofpower is the scale of peace. The same balance would be preserved were all the world destitute of arms, for all would be alike; but since some will not, others dare not lay them aside. And while a single nation refuses to lay them down, it is proper that all should keep them up. Horrid mischief would ensue were one-half the world deprived of the use of them; for while avarice and ambition have a place in the heart of man, the weak will become a prey to the strong. The history of every age and nation establishes these truths, and facts need but little arguments when they prove themselves."

 - Thomas Paine, "Thoughts on Defensive War" in Pennsylvania Magazine, July 1775

"The Constitution shall never be construed to prevent the people of the United States who are peaceable citizens from keeping their own arms."

- Samuel Adams, Massachusetts Ratifying Convention, 1788

"The right of the citizens to keep and bear arms has justly been considered, as the palladium of the liberties of a republic; since it offers a strong moral check against the usurpation and arbitrary power of rulers; and will generally, even if these are successful in the first instance, enable the people to resist and triumph over them."

- Joseph Story, Commentaries on the Constitution of the United States, 1833

"What, Sir, is the use of a militia? It is to prevent the establishment of a standing army, the bane of liberty .... Whenever Governments mean to invade the rights and liberties of the people, they always attempt to destroy the militia, in order to raise an army upon their ruins."

- Rep. Elbridge Gerry of Massachusetts, I Annals of Congress 750, August 17, 1789

"For it is a truth, which the experience of ages has attested, that the people are always most in danger when the means of injuring their rights are in the possession of those of whom they entertain the least suspicion."

- Alexander Hamilton, Federalist No. 25, December 21, 1787

"If the representatives of the people betray their constituents, there is then no resource left but in the exertion of that original right of self-defense which is paramount to all positive forms of government, and which against the usurpations of the national rulers, may be exerted with infinitely better prospect of success than against those of the rulers of an individual state. In a single state, if the persons intrusted with supreme power become usurpers, the different parcels, subdivisions, or districts of which it consists, having no distinct government in each, can take no regular measures for defense. The citizens must rush tumultuously to arms, without concert, without system, without resource; except in their courage and despair."

 - Alexander Hamilton, Federalist No. 28

"[I]f circumstances should at any time oblige the government to form an army of any magnitude that army can never be formidable to the liberties of the people while there is a large body of citizens, little, if at all, inferior to them in discipline and the use of arms, who stand ready to defend their own rights and those of their fellow-citizens. This appears to me the only substitute that can be devised for a standing army, and the best possible security against it, if it should exist."

 - Alexander Hamilton, Federalist No. 28, January 10, 1788

If we don't start standing up and defending our Constitution we will lose it.

Chapter 14 – Challenge

John Witherspoon

Signer of the Declaration of Independence, Clergyman and President of Princeton University

"While we give praise to God, the Supreme Disposer of all events, for His interposition on our behalf, let us guard against the dangerous error of trusting in, or boasting of, an arm of flesh ... If your cause is just, if your principles are pure, and if your conduct is prudent, you need not fear the multitude of opposing hosts.

"What follows from this? That he is the best friend to American liberty, who is most sincere and active in promoting true and undefiled religion, and who sets himself with the greatest firmness to bear down profanity and immorality of every kind.

"Whoever is an avowed enemy of God, I scruple not to call him an enemy of his country."

--Sermon at Princeton University, "The Dominion of Providence over the Passions of Men," May 17, 1776.

I have put a lot of prayer and work in this book. Not one word is out of hatred or bigotry. Every single word in the book is out of love. Love of God, family, and country. You may agree with parts or all of the book, or you may disagree with parts or all of the book. I can't control that. I can only plant the seeds.

I wrote this book not for fame or fortune. If it does like my other 3 books I'll be lucky if I break even. I certainly won't receive any fame from it, maybe notoriety. I wrote this book because our country is in trouble. Someone has to do something to wake people up.

I wrote this book because I have children and grandchildren and I want them to grow up in a free country. To have the same opportunities I had.

I wrote this book because I believe in my heart and soul God wanted me to. I didn't want to. I know what kind of hate mail and comments I will receive, but I believe someone had to step up and say it.

I challenge each and every person who reads this book to pray for our country. I challenge you to do your part in making it great again. I challenge to find your inner John F. Kennedy and "ask not what your country can do for you, but what can you do for your country."

I challenge you no matter how good of a parent you are, be a better one. No matter how good of a citizen you are, be a better one. No matter how good of a child, brother, sister, employee, student, be a better one.

I challenge you to spend more time in your Bible. Spend more time talking to God. Spend more time in prayer. Spend more time pleasing God and less time pleasing man.

Spend more time seeking God's will in your life and less time seeking your will.

I challenge you to stop the hate. We can and will disagree, but we don't have to hate.

I can be reached at WeOweItToOurChildren@aol.com for questions comments.

I leave you with this:

John 3:16King James Version (KJV)

16 For God so loved the world, that he gave his only begotten Son, that whosoever believeth in him should not perish, but have everlasting life.

He surrendered His life for you, live your life for Him.

www.ingramcontent.com/pod-product-compliance
Lightning Source LLC
LaVergne TN
LVHW051514080426
835509LV00017B/2058